SMART START II

SMART START II
WHY STANDARDS MATTER

Patte Barth and Ruth Mitchell

Illustrations by Jon Chester

fulcrum resources
Golden, Colorado

Library of Congress Cataloging-in-Publication Data
    Barth, Patte.
        Smart start II : why standards matter / Patte Barth and Ruth Mitchell.
            p. cm.
        Includes bibliographical references and index.
        ISBN 1-55591-850-6 (pbk.)
        1. Education, Elementary — United States.
    2. Educational change — United States. 3. Education,
    Elementary — United States — Evaluation. I. Title: Smart
    start 2. II. Mitchell, Ruth, 1933– III. Barth, Patte. Smart
    start. IV. Title.
        LA219 .B37 2001   2001001720
        372.973—dc21

Printed in the United States of America
0 9 8 7 6 5 4 3 2 1

Book production by Pauline Brown, Pebble Graphics

Fulcrum Resources
16100 Table Mountain Parkway, Suite 300
Golden, Colorado 80403
(800) 992-2908 • (303) 277-1623
www.fulcrum-resources.com

CONTENTS

PREFACE

WHY SMART START II?

W HEN THE FIRST EDITION of *Smart Start* was published in 1992, the national standards were in the future. That future is here. Nationally, standards have been adopted by the professional subject-area groups. In addition, forty-nine of the fifty states have their own standards documents, and many cities, counties, and regions also have standards. One national organization, the National Center on Education and the Economy, produced standards that have influenced many state and local standards: the *New Standards Performance Standards*. Forty-seven of the states have assessments to gauge how students are doing.[1] Standards have been introduced to parents in PTA meetings and are the content of innumerable professional development workshops for teachers.

What does this mean? What is standards-based education and what does it look like? These questions need answers because, as we forecast when we wrote the first edition of *Smart Start* in 1991, the landscape in education is different now. Dimly apprehended then, standards-based education has come into focus. This necessitates a new edition of *Smart Start*.

A new edition of a book raises the question, how different is it from the original? If I read the first *Smart Start*, do I need to read *Smart Start II*? We want to assure potential readers that in its bedrock beliefs and principles, the book remains the same: the core of schooling is academic learning, and the focus is on academic content and achievement. All children can learn to high levels, and it is the business of schools to

see that they do. But *Smart Start II* constructs a specific vision of elementary education on these foundations—specific, because it is supported by a framework, the standards, that was simply not available at the beginning of the 1990s.

Standards have changed much in elementary education, and more changes are on the way. Because there are now clear goals—for example, children are expected to read and write by the end of first grade—instruction has a focus. It is significant that in the first edition of *Smart Start* we frequently referred to our list of expectations ("What Twelve-Year-Olds Should Know and Be Able to Do") as curriculum. We would not make that mistake now. Standards are the goals, the expectations, the WHAT of education; curriculum and instruction are the HOW.

This book, like the standards themselves, does not prescribe HOW, although we provide examples of successful classrooms. There are many roads to the standards, and we discuss some of them in terms of the changes in the conditions of education, but none has priority in all cases. Reform proposals such as enlisting charter schools and mainstreaming special education students receive considerable attention in the press. Yet their merits should be judged on whether or not they help students meet standards.

Along with standards has come accountability—in many cases the center of politicians' interest in education. Not only students but also schools are now being held accountable for student achievement. These developments of the 1990s have affected the entire landscape of elementary education, from the revision of thinking about testing young children, to the retention of fourth–graders who can't read.

Almost as profound as the changes that standards have initiated are the changes effected by computer technology. Students in first grade are preparing reports on word processors and sixth-graders surf the Net. How can we make sure that this potentially loose cannon is a positive, not a destructive, force?

There is also a dark shadow over elementary education that did not loom to the same extent in the early 1990s. Incidents of violence in elementary schools, shootings by students, and attacks on students and teachers all have created an atmosphere in which parents are justifiably worried about the safety in schools. The availability of both guns and drugs, as well as precocious sexuality fostered by the media, have ruined the image of elementary school as a protected haven from the outside world.

These factors—the standards and their dramatic effects on all sectors of education, together with accountability, technology, and concerns about school safety—should argue forcefully that a book on elementary education at the beginning of the new millennium must be different from one written in the early 1990s. But *Smart Start* and *Smart Start II* are not fundamentally at odds. Both books are based on the same beliefs and principles, which, as synonyms are not infinite, must sometimes be expressed in the same words. Some reading–list items are the same: the world's great myths and legends, the Bible as literature, Shakespeare, and Homer do not change. But much of *Smart Start II* contains different material, so that these two books are not interchangeable. They are books of their time—one forecasting somewhat indistinctly the revolutions of the 1990s, and one explaining the effects of those revolutions and their consequences for the first decade of the twenty-first century.

The readers for whom this book is intended are those who care about the shape and direction of elementary education. Parents, grandparents, and caretakers of children entering elementary school will find the book helpful in explaining what they should expect. This book will help teachers to see how elementary education prepares students for secondary school and for life, although it won't supplant the place of curriculum guides or even the standards themselves. It will help administrators—principals and central office personnel—to make policy for good elementary education in their districts. It will perform almost the same function for community and school-board members, who need to understand the purposes of elementary school but do not need to be concerned with the everyday details. This book should have a place in the libraries of education schools to help prospective teachers (and their teachers) focus on the essentials of elementary education. It should be in the hands of legislative aides and businesspeople concerned with state-level policy to motivate schools with appropriate carrots and sticks to serve children well in their most vulnerable educational years.

Smart Start II brings together in one place a brief history of standards development and an explanation of what standards are and are not, with a discussion of controversies surrounding them; standards in English/language arts, mathematics, history/social studies, and science at grades 1, 4, and 6; and descriptions of safe and secure conditions in elementary schools that will enable students to attain the standards. This book includes a discussion of the value of technology and how that value can be ensured, and recommendations for policies appropriate to various groups interested in elementary education.

Our ideas are based on reading and research, but also to a great extent on experience introducing standards to educational personnel and to parent and community groups. Those experiences have made clear the need for the kind of extended explanation that only a book can provide.

Smart Start II will provide an accessible guide to good elementary education. It should reassure all who care about our future—our children—that standards-based education is the smartest of smart starts.

NOTES

1. American Federation of Teachers, *Making Standards Matter, 1999,* 7. In this publication, the District of Columbia and Puerto Rico are counted as states for a total of fifty-two. Three states (Montana, Iowa, and North Dakota) have no plans for statewide assessments aligned with standards.

INTRODUCTION

STANDARDS-BASED ELEMENTARY EDUCATION

I N THE 1990s, educational reformers in the United States began a movement unlike any other in the long history of educational efforts to get schooling to match promises with results. It is unlike other reform efforts because it affects every part of the educational system by bringing about change at the core where all reforms must stand or fall: the classroom.

Standards-based education is based on a simple premise: tell everyone publicly what all students should know and be able to do; at certain points test whether they know and can do it; and let schools figure out how to ensure that students know and can do what is required by the standards. Simple, but profound in scope and consequences.

Standards imply a cascade of changes, from the boardroom to the playground: changes in the distribution of resources—time, money, supplies, equipment, personnel—changes in governance structures, and changes in attitude and emphasis. This book will explore how standards are bringing about these changes in elementary schools, which have been the first to adopt standards and which have made the most progress in practice. It will convey what standards-based education in elementary schools looks like and feels like.

EXCELLENCE AND EQUITY UNITED

In the 1980s and 1990s, U.S. education was seen as failing on several fronts: U.S. students fell far behind their international counterparts on tests of mathematics and science, students dropped out of high school at alarming rates, and grim jokes were made about high school graduates who couldn't read their diplomas as employers groused about having to provide basic education to their young employees. Perhaps most devastating of all, a great divide in achievement had appeared between students who attended well-financed, mainly suburban school districts, and those confined to less wealthy urban and rural districts. It was apparent that a fine ideal of nineteenth-century America, the common school, no longer operated at the end of the twentieth century.

The common school, the dream of Horace Mann, would ensure the continuation and strengthening of democracy through a well-educated citizenry. But when students were so severely tracked that they went into the school through one door, but separated immediately afterward and never met in a class again, they could not be said to have a common body of knowledge. Those in the bottom tracks, who would probably drop out and never receive a diploma, much less a postsecondary education, were essentially wasted material, not only as citizens, but also as workers lost to the developing "knowledge economy."

The reform of the last two decades of the twentieth century therefore had two motivating forces: to ensure that U.S. education was rigorous enough to make the United States economically and educationally equal to any other country, and to ensure that all students could participate in a technologically sophisticated economy, both for their own sake and for that of the nation as a whole. No human resources should be wasted and no lives stunted for lack of education.

ELEMENTARY SCHOOL
THROUGH COMMENCEMENT

Education should give people the tools to control their lives. Albert Shanker, the late president of the American Federation of Teachers, used to say that American education has always worked, but only for the top 20 percent of students. These few students who traditionally succeed are given those tools almost as a birthright. They get into the high reading groups (the bluebirds, they used to be called) in elementary school, learn algebra in middle school, know when to take the PSAT and the SAT, are helped by counselors and parents to file college applications, and sail on to college and career. They choose their futures—doctor, lawyer, entrepreneur, computer engineer, software developer, stockbroker, investment banker.

The other students are controlled by their fate; they don't control it. If a child does not read well by the end of elementary school, there are few choices—certainly not college and therefore not any of the careers that build on college. Before the 1970s there was no economic penalty for school failure: strong arms could make a decent living for a family from work in factories, mines, and on farms. No longer. In the early twenty-first century, few options are open to anyone who hasn't had some college, and choices are best for those who make it all the way to commencement. The knowledge economy is merciless.[1] It has no use for people whose qualifications consist only of a willing body.

For students who graduate from college, a large measure of control over their lives is in their hands. They have been introduced to what Josiah Royce called "the tools the race has found indispensable"—the heritage of history, literature, scientific knowledge, and philosophy that places everyday concerns within a context larger than themselves. Their commencement ceremony signals the beginning of a productive adult life.

For future college graduates, commencement begins early, with preschool and kindergarten, with early exposure to print, with counting cookies and slices of pizza, with questions asked and answered. Successful graduates grasped the tools of control when they first stepped into a classroom.

Standards-based education promises to enable all students to grasp those tools. It is designed to achieve both rigor and equity, the two aims of the present reform. It does so by establishing clear public standards and insisting that all students meet them. No exceptions, no excuses. If we keep standards-based education on the right track and don't let shortsighted decisions cut off its potential, it is possible that all students will be able to make their own life choices.

FOCUS ON ACADEMIC LEARNING

Because of our emphasis on academic learning—an emphasis increasingly shared in schools and districts around the country—we are less concerned with the social and physical aspects of elementary education than a comprehensive discussion would be. Excellent work on the affective and physical development of children is easily available, and we acknowledge its importance. Our focus is students' academic learning and how the standards foster it.

But this emphasis does not mean that we are either ignorant of or are ignoring the effects of poverty, family disintegration, and adult irresponsibility on the ability of students to learn. We offer data on these problems, which are as intense now as when we wrote the first edition of *Smart Start* in 1991. But we also offer data on schools where students achieve academically despite horrendous social difficulties. Schools in high-poverty districts with all the impediments of transience and English as a second language have scored as high as advantaged suburban districts on tests—and sometimes higher. The job of the school, we argue, is to take children where they are and help them to learn to high standards, no matter what it takes.

We also offer data to show that focus on academics reduces social problems in schools. Where children are achieving, always striving to read the next book and write a more effective paper, the need for psychoactive medications decreases, problem behavior diminishes, and violence recedes.

BUT ARE OUR CHILDREN SAFE?

The primary mission of schools is the academic development of children. But schools are also responsible for the health and safety of their charges during school hours. In the 1990s several deadly events took place on school grounds that have made safety more than an idle concern, especially for parents.

Some statistical perspective is needed first. Children are significantly safer while at school than they are on the streets, in a moving car, or even in their homes. Violent crime and thefts against young people are still infrequent inside our school buildings, certainly more so than outside them, and have been steadily *decreasing* over the decade. Weapon-related injuries in our high schools are virtually unchanged since the mid-1970s. And fortunately for our youngest students, acts of violence are almost unknown in elementary schools.[2]

But small risk in reality does little to alleviate adult fears when a six–year–old is shot to death by a classmate or a madman opens fire on a playground. These horrific crimes make it hard for us to be comforted by statistics. A person afraid of flying knows rationally that air travel has the best record for avoiding accidents but reacts emotionally to the dismal odds for survival if the plane crashes. So it is with guns in schools: it's a rare occurrence, but we also know that when it happens the outcome is likely to be devastating. The perception of risk can itself disrupt the educational mission of schools. We need to pay attention when our youngsters, despite the decline in school violence, feel more threatened at school now than ever before.[3]

For both real and imagined reasons, schools have to think about the unthinkable. They need to secure their buildings and do everything they can to prevent disaster. At the same time, they need to avoid feeding children's fears by seeming overly cautious. It's a delicate balancing act. Until legislators muster up the courage to pass reasonable gun laws, schools will have to do their best without.

The schools we visited for this book are all conscious of the need to create a safe and comforting environment. Some, as we will show, are located in crime-ridden neighborhoods where walking to and from school can be treacherous. Keeping out danger is just one of their concerns, however. They must also find ways to keep the chaos many children live with from intruding on the classroom.

WHERE IS DISCIPLINE?

Successful schools manage to create a safe and orderly atmosphere for children by generating a feeling of shared purpose among adults and students alike. When children are doing interesting work, know the goals for that work, and can trust the adults in the building to support them, discipline problems are rare. Social theorist Alfie Kohn identifies "three Cs" for student motivation that contribute to a productive and safe school environment: *Content*, giving students work that's worth doing; *Community*, making students feel safe and supported in their learning; and *Choice*, granting students some control over their learning.[4]

Small schools help. Fewer than one in ten small schools report serious crimes, compared to one in three schools with large student populations.[5] Certainly, small schools are more hospitable to creating the sense of community that Alfie Kohn describes. Simply more students are known to more adults. It's hard for anyone to remain invisible for long.

We have seen large, overcrowded schools where maintaining discipline is like keeping the lid on a boiling pot. On the other hand, we also visited an elementary school with an astounding 1,300 students where the children were well behaved, happy, and completely engaged in their classes.

A popular response to health and safety concerns has been "zero tolerance" rules that govern everything from weapon and drug possession to threatening speech. While these rules seem attractive on the surface, their enforcement has led to such bizarre incidents as students being expelled for sharing cough drops or having table knives in their lunch bags.[6] By interfering with common sense, zero tolerance paradoxically begins to appear arbitrary and unfair. As a result, such policies are attracting the attention of civil rights groups. Worse, zero tolerance sends a message to students that the administration of rules takes precedence over the just treatment of the individual, leaving students to feel they have no recourse and no control.

The bottom line with zero tolerance rules is that they don't work. According to psychologists Russ Skiba and Reece Peterson, "Virtually no data suggest that zero tolerance policies reduce school violence, and some data suggest that certain strategies … may create emotional harm or encourage students to drop out."[7]

In researching this book, we visited several elementary schools where everyone understood the rules as part and parcel of the work, but the work is what motivated compliance. These schools exemplified content, community, and choice. Teachers, administrators, parents, and students knew the standards and could see how their efforts contributed to achievement. We saw first-graders use scoring guides for assignments to evaluate their own work and make adjustments to get a better score if needed. We watched a class of fourth-graders and their teacher analyze their scores on the district assessment (for the whole class, names were anonymous), and together they identified areas of strength and weakness in order to plan what skills the class would focus on over the next nine weeks. We did not see fidgeting, acting out, daydreaming, or the other distractions that have become so familiar in U.S. classrooms.

By focusing on their core mission and doing it well, these schools also succeed at minimizing discipline problems. The sense of shared academic purpose among adults and students fosters a climate in which no one feels neglected, confused, or left out. In these places, the school, at least, does not contribute to the anger and alienation that many children feel and that leads a few to actual violence. We can ask schools for no more than that.

THE SHAPE OF THE BOOK

In chapter one, we tell the story of Andrew as an emblem of the common fate of children in an educational system that did not know its purpose. We contrast poor Andrew's fate with the exuberance of children in an inner-city school who can read in kindergarten and glory in their skill.

Our second chapter sketches the history and development of standards, why the U.S. needed to establish academic standards, what they are—and are not, and how they are working in elementary schools around the country. It will discuss the controversy surrounding some of the national and state standards and why they have met with opposition in some places.

Our third chapter sets out standards in literacy (reading and writing), mathematics, history/social studies, and science. At what grade levels? That isn't as easy to answer as it seems it should be. The national standards and the National Assessment of Educational Progress (NAEP) were written for grade 4 and grade 8, with high school standards varying among grades 10, 11, and 12 (or age seventeen in the case of NAEP). If the national standards were all we had, we would then be trying to stretch our usual K–6 definition of elementary school on a Procrustean bed: should elementary school be defined as going up to grade 8, or should we lop a piece off and say it ends at grade 4?

However, a large number of states and cities have standards at all grade levels, kindergarten through grade 12. It is therefore possible to retain the usual definition of elementary school as kindergarten through grade 6 and list standards in English/language arts, mathematics, and science for the end of elementary school: here is what students should know and be able to do as they go into middle or junior high school.

We could synthesize a selection of state and local standards and list standards for the end of each grade, K–6, but that would be tedious and unnecessary. This book is not intended as a compendium of standards—there are excellent publications that provide exhaustive collections of standards[8]—but as an introduction to their content and use.

We shall therefore list standards at the end of grade 1, grade 4, and grade 6. Grade 1 is the end of the first two years of schooling and has a new importance in view of the emphasis on early literacy. Grade 4 is significant because in some large city school districts (Chicago, New York, and Washington, D.C.), students may not proceed to grade 5 if they haven't met the standards—that is, passed the assessment—at grade 4. Grade 6 is typically the culminating year of elementary school.

We should also explain why chapter three includes standards in only four subject areas: English/language arts, mathematics, history/social studies, and science. Why not in the arts and world languages, as in the first edition of *Smart Start*? Or in health and physical education, as in many states? Because we want to focus on essentials.

The dismal performance of U.S. students at grades 4 and 8 on the NAEP and on international assessments such as the Third International Mathematics and Science Survey (TIMSS) makes clear that the elementary curriculum does not go deep enough in basic subjects such as literacy and mathematics. The curriculum focus on these subjects is reinforced by the fact that the arts and world languages are not usually tested by states and districts—many test only literacy and mathematics. But we certainly support the arts and world languages as essential for educated people, and so we have listed the relevant standards in Appendix C, including a large part of section three from the first edition of *Smart Start*.

With a rationale for standards and the standards themselves in hand, in chapter four we describe why we aren't meeting these standards now. We offer four principles on which our vision of standards-based elementary education is based and explain why they are fundamental. These principles are:

- all children can learn, so there should be no achievement gaps between ethnic and socioeconomic groups;

- learning should be connected and grow from children's experiences, respecting their backgrounds and their heritages;

- student learning depends on good teaching; and

- instruction must be balanced between theoretical extremes.

The discussion of these principles will be supported with the work of such researchers as Lauren Resnick, Fred Newmann and Gary Wehlage, and the DataWorks team in California, all of whom agree that students should be challenged to work with concepts and think deeply about applications of knowledge, not simply memorize facts or spend endless hours on basic skills. The final portion of the chapter will help readers to tread a neutral path between the armies fighting the reading and math wars.

In chapter five we confront the question of ways to get to the standards. We approach it by focusing on literacy and how it is achieved in two dramatically different ways. In one vignette we show how some schools with high populations of poor and minority students get them reading and comprehending what they read by the end of kindergarten; in another we show how literacy is achieved by "accountable talk," in a district where customs and backgrounds are quite different. The point? How students learn to read and write is less important than that they do so early and fluently.

Chapter six discusses the issues presented by technology both in school and at home, for students and for teachers. In it, we point out that computer and information technology will dominate the lives of the students now in elementary schools in ways we cannot imagine. Five years ago we used e-mail perhaps, but we weren't dependent on it for a large proportion of our daily affairs. Now it is central to our lives, and the pace of change is only going to accelerate.

Chapter seven tackles the issues that loom over standards-based education and indeed threaten the reform it brings—accountability and assessment. What kind of testing should be done and how often should it occur? Is testing harmful to young children? Should teachers teach to the test? How should state and district authorities choose tests? This chapter should be reassuring to both parents and school personnel, for it will help them thread their way through the testing maze.

Finally, in chapter eight we offer recommendations for the adults outside the classroom who can make a difference—administrators, parents, university faculties, and state and local elected officials. Elementary students cannot reach standards without the informed support of everyone involved. Well-educated students will guarantee all of us the future we desire.

Now let's meet Andrew.

NOTES

1. Friedman, *Lexus and the Olive Tree*, on globalization provides a lively explanation of the effects of a worldwide information-based economy on all sectors of the population.

2. U.S. Department of Education, *Annual Report on School Safety–October 1998*, and National Center for Injury Prevention and Control, Centers for Disease Control and Prevention, 1997.

3. U.S. Department of Education, *Annual Report on School Safety.*

4. Brandt, "Punished by Rewards?" Alfie Kohn has become one of the most visible critics of the standards movement. Yet he is the first to agree that all students need meaningful and challenging content—a point on which he and standards advocates like us are in complete agreement.

5. U.S. Department of Education, *Annual Report on School Safety.*

6. Skiba and Peterson, "Dark Side of Zero Tolerance."

7. Ibid.

8. Listed in Appendix C.

SMART START II

CHAPTER ONE

ANDREW'S FATE

THE ABSENCE OF STANDARDS in U.S. education meant traveling without a map. We didn't know where we were supposed to be going. We also didn't know where we were. Students were left to haphazardly strike out in many directions. Those with luck and motivation managed by following the route of some savvy pathfinder—sometimes a teacher, a school counselor, often a parent—who could lead them to college and careers. But the journey itself could be fraught with missed turns and disasters. Lacking an experienced guide, even the most tenacious student could end up part of an academic Donner Party.

If this sounds like exaggeration, consider the example of Andrew. When Andrew started kindergarten, most of his classmates could recognize letters and a few were already reading. He had little experience with books. But he liked the stories his mother told him at night and would act them out with his own embellishments. By the end of the school year, Andrew was singing the alphabet song. He especially loved to roll out the *el-em-en-o-pee*, even if he couldn't quite distinguish between all the letters. His teacher told Andrew's mother that it would come with time.

Andrew's first-grade teacher believed it was wrong to push young children. Andrew and his classmates played lots of letter and number games and spent considerable effort decorating their journals with drawings. His teacher liked having Andrew in her class. She told his

mother that he had a great imagination and was very popular with the other children.

Andrew was placed with a group of other nonreaders. On worksheet after worksheet they matched letters to beginning and ending sounds and followed along as the teacher pointed at the words in big books about Bob and Spot. At the end of second grade, his teacher was pleased that Andrew was now able to independently read books such as *Hop on Pop*. She thought it was good progress for a year's work, particularly when she considered where he was when she got him as a student the previous fall. Most of his classmates had moved on to chapter books.

Andrew struggled with his classwork in third and fourth grade. He watched as students who quickly finished their worksheets were allowed to attack the daily math "brainteasers" or were rewarded with time on the computer. Andrew couldn't seem to focus on twenty fill-in-the-blank problems in a row. His mind kept wandering to the X-Men, Nintendo, and football. Even though he knew it would mean yet another missed recess if he didn't finish his work, he couldn't stop himself from daydreaming or talking.

Andrew was falling farther and farther behind academically. Not only that, by fifth grade he was considered a "problem." What had been friendly and imaginative behavior in a six-year-old was now viewed as disruptive to the class. When his mother asked about Andrew's prospects in middle school, his sixth-grade teacher just shook her head. She filed a recommendation for Andrew to be enrolled in the remedial math and English courses.

Children like Andrew are in elementary schools all over this country. Because their teachers lack a clear set of expectations that all their students are expected to meet, they continue to pass children on, happy enough with any progress they make and believing that knowledge and skill will come to the slow learners at some ambiguous later time. Unfortunately for a lot of children, later turns out to be never. Many of these children are in so-called good schools—"good" because enough children in them score high on standardized tests to shore up the school's average, concealing the nonachievers. But whole schools of Andrews exist, especially in communities of high poverty. In these schools teachers often hesitate to demand too much of their students out of sincere but ultimately misdirected sympathy for their already difficult lives.

We can admire the good intentions of these teachers. After all, we want our younger students to be in the hands of caring adults. But when their compassion manifests in low academic expectations, they are in fact doing harm to precisely those students they want to help and who need their help the most.

It's easy to predict what kind of high school career a student like Andrew will have. Being placed in low-tracked math and reading courses in middle school immediately rules out eighth-grade algebra, which in the scheme of high school mathematics, rules out any possibility for calculus. There's only the remotest chance that he will take enough high-level math and English in high school to be able to perform college-level work after graduating, assuming of course that he even graduates.[1] Indeed, middle school usually presents students like Andrew with just two choices: become invisible or become a trouble-maker. It's a bleak future for a twelve- year-old to face. And it results from the failure of elementary school to provide the proper academic foundation.

These lost young people can be male or female, of any race or nationality. Again, the data show that poor and minority children are disproportionately represented in their ranks. National Assessment of Educational Progress results in reading and mathematics reveal that far too few U.S. elementary students are meeting standards in reading and mathematics. Fewer than one in three fourth-graders are proficient readers, and only one in five are proficient in mathematics.[2] Within this overall mediocre performance exist appalling gaps between groups of students. Sadly, our school corridors are not yet swept clean of the ghosts of racism and classism.

A MOB OF YOUNG READERS

It doesn't have to be this way. We visited another kindergarten class in another school. This one was located in a midsize urban district in eastern Pennsylvania. The school had a majority of African-American and Latino students. Nearly all of the students were eligible for subsidized lunches. Teachers could expect that more than half their students in the fall would not be there in the spring, but would be replaced by new faces. The highly transient neighborhood was also a haven for drug users and traffickers.

Visitors must ring a bell to enter the locked steel doors to the century-old building. As the doors slammed shut behind us, the outside neighborhood disappeared as well. Despite its age, the school was well maintained and clean. Inside was a safe place where all adults are trusted and are there to help students learn. These children didn't know us. Yet we didn't enter a classroom or walk through a hallway without a student stopping us, politely of course, to ask for help with their work.

Nothing prepared us for the kindergarten class. The principal escorting us there mentioned that it was probably close to reading time, which brought to our minds quiet images of libraries and reading rooms. No such thing. As soon as we entered the room, we were mobbed by eager five-year-olds waving books and begging "Can I read to you?" "Me first, please!" All we could do, quite literally, was stop in our tracks, sit down, and let the children read.

One at a time (surprising that with all this exuberance there was order), the children read to us, some of them sitting on our laps. They read published books and short mimeographed stories they had illustrated themselves. They needed help with some, like a book on dinosaurs one little boy was interested in. But most they read on their own quite masterfully, stopping occasionally to sound out an unfamiliar word, and they could answer questions we asked about what they had just read.

It was hard for these kindergartners to let us leave. It was hard for us too, for we had never encountered such energy in children proud that they had cracked the code to reading.

We must emphasize that these are the children who in most school districts would be the least likely to achieve—poor, minority, from single-parent households, from unstable homes, crack babies. But the burden of bad odds did not dissuade this principal, even if it gave her a tough sale to make to her staff.

One year earlier, she sent all her kindergarten teachers to intensive literacy training provided by the district as part of its commitment to reading. The teacher whose classroom we had just left had been a doubter who, like Andrew's first-grade teacher, believed it was wrong to push children too hard before they were "ready." The principal forced her to attend the training and to implement the strategies in her class.

Do we even need to mention that this teacher is now a passionate convert? Results are hard to argue with, especially when they are this dramatic. As further proof, the kindergartners whose teachers committed to the literacy program performed better on the same standardized reading assessment than first-graders whose teachers had not yet participated. The school as a whole went up ninety points on the state assessment in reading and mathematics in one year and received more than $14,000 in state incentive money.

What did school give these young kindergartners that Andrew missed? First of all, the district made a decision—known to teachers, parents, and students alike—that all children would be reading by the end of first grade, so the earlier they started the better. They also had standards aligned with their goal that provided clear signposts along the way to literacy. Had this been the policy in Andrew's school, his first teachers would not have allowed his lack of progress, and his mother would have known to demand more.

The Pennsylvania district also put its money where its mouth was by committing resources for professional development for teachers and extra support for students. In contrast, Andrew's teachers were not prepared in strategies to accelerate learning in students who start behind. In fact, their philosophy of not "pushing" younger students was probably formed in education school.

The success of their kindergartners notwithstanding, the Pennsylvania district administrators still have a lot of work cut out for them. They must sustain the progress being made by their emerging readers. At the same time, they have an obligation to older students who didn't get the same rigorous preparation in the early grades. And they must find the means to replicate their progress in literacy with other subjects, especially mathematics.

But the district is now committed to aligning all its classroom work with standards. We will outline those standards in chapter three, but first we need to explain how, why, and when standards came into U.S. education.

NOTES

1. Adelman, *Answers in the Tool Box.*

2. National Center for Education Statistics, *NAEP 1998 Reading Report,* and *NAEP 1996 Mathematics Report Card.*

CHAPTER TWO

STANDARDS: WHAT IS ALL THE FUSS ABOUT?

EDUCATION IN THE United States is plagued by lack of communication. There are so many layers of authority, from the federal government in Washington, D.C. (not much authority), to local school boards (a great deal more), with the state education authorities in between, all requiring compliance with regulations, giving advice, or changing policies (sometimes without warning). None of them seems to take responsibility for communicating clearly to the teachers on the front line in the classrooms or the parents of the children in the classrooms about the learning that is expected. Standards are a major change in U.S. education. They need clear explanation and they haven't had much of it. Without it, standards can seem like just another educational fad on the level of open classrooms, cooperative learning, or left-brain, right-brain learning.

Consequently, when we meet with groups to help teachers to align their practice to standards or to help parents to understand what this means, a series of questions is usually fired at us:[1]

- What are standards?

- Why do we need standards?

- Where did standards come from?

- Who wrote these standards?

- How can standards make a difference?

Because these questions are so frequently asked, this chapter's brief history and explanation of standards is organized around them. In most cases, the answers apply to all levels of schooling, although we will focus particularly on elementary school.

WHAT ARE STANDARDS?

Standards are public statements of what students should know and be able to do. The important word to focus on is *public*. Because they are available for everyone to see, standards are potent tools for equity. A parent can look at what is expected in mathematics, for example, at grade 4, and can ask the child's teacher what is being done to ensure that the child meets those standards. Children in grade 4 should be making, reading, and interpreting graphs.[2] Does the curriculum include practice with graphs? Does the child's homework include making graphs or perhaps collecting information for a graph—say, of shoe size among a group of people?

The simple answer is that standards lay out what students should know and be able to do at certain points in their school experience. Standards are not the same thing as curriculum. Unlike textbooks, standards documents cannot be directly taught from. Standards describe the ends of education, the goals, the expectations. Curriculum is the means of getting to those ends. Because standards are the destination, any number of paths can get students there. Thus standards do not restrict choices, they open them up.

WHY DO WE
NEED STANDARDS?

Until we began to formulate standards in the early 1990s, U.S. schools had no public criteria by which to judge students' academic performance. Andrew's teachers and parents had no document they could point to that would tell them what he should know and be able to do. The student who got the highest grade in the class, or on a test, was the best student and could become the valedictorian in the high school graduating class by accumulating high grades.

But the best in one school was not necessarily the best in another. An A in one teacher's class would be a B or C in another teacher's class. The criteria by which students were judged, about what constitutes good student work, was essentially private, locked in teachers' heads.

Furthermore, there was no consensus about what students should learn, so that a high school diploma could mean ability to run a lathe or to translate Virgil into English. The common element was seat time, hours spent in courses adding up to the so-called Carnegie unit count. That was all a diploma meant—it conveyed no sense that a student had mastered a body of knowledge and skills.[3]

The educational system was doing quite well, thank you, at what it was designed to do for the Industrial Age. School provided rich and challenging content to a handful of students, typically those who came into the system with the advantages of family support and understanding of the educational system. These young people would go on to the elite universities and become the leaders and upper-echelon administrators in business, government, industry, and the professions. The other 80 percent would come into the educational system without understanding how it worked and how to manipulate it, and they would exit essentially unchanged except for minimal literacy.

Until about 1970 there were jobs for a large proportion of that 80 percent. The assembly lines that made the United States rich and its population prosperous in the mid-twentieth century needed workers who could read, write, and compute just well enough to handle their routine jobs. The economic boom following World War II brought middle-class status to formerly low-paying blue-collar jobs. But at the end of their work shifts, these workers used to race each other out of the factories to the cars they could now buy, so eager were they to leave their boring jobs.

Over the last three decades, assembly-line jobs have been rapidly disappearing. The evolving new economy values brains over brawn. Policy makers and business leaders were the first to recognize that the United States needed smart workers if we were to retain our economic position. Yet the public education system continued to educate the few to high levels in a world that didn't need the physical strength, which was the majority's main qualification. The schools were producing bolt-tighteners for assembly lines, although manufacturing is increasingly done by robots operated by technicians who read computer screens to command them.

The education system needed a complete rethinking of its role. Beginning in the 1980s, that rethinking was forced on the system from outside. Alarms were first sounded in 1983 with the publication of *A Nation at Risk*, the report of the National Commission on Excellence in Education on behalf of the new U.S. Department of Education. This document argued persuasively that the United States faced a downward spiral into third-world country status if U.S. students were not better educated. Nearly every state responded promptly to the report's call by mandating more coursework in math, science, English, and social studies as a condition for high school graduation.

The reforms that followed *A Nation at Risk* failed to make a significant difference in achievement, however. There are two reasons for this. First, the education system responded to the higher graduation requirements with the hydralike proliferation of courses for different students. The reforms specified subject areas, but never the content of those subjects. Thus, some students were enrolled in "consumer math" while others took calculus. In "business English" students wrote letters and memos, while their peers in AP English wrote critical analyses of Shakespeare. Students were exposed to more years of mathematics and English, but most of them were still denied challenging subject matter.

Second, the reforms bypassed elementary schools. Students still entered high school with widely different academic experiences resulting from their placement in ability groups in the primary grades. For the majority, even if algebra were open to them, they had not been adequately prepared to succeed.

The education system proved itself remarkably resistant to substantial change. By the late 1980s, outside pressure would come from very high up.

WHERE DID STANDARDS COME FROM?

President George Bush called all of the nation's governors to an emergency education summit in 1989. It was only the third time in U.S. history that the president had convened the governors to address a national crisis and the first to concern education. Every governor attended, with the exception of Governor Perpich of Minnesota, who was detained at the last minute by a miners strike. The nation's top leaders were telling the education establishment that the system must educate successfully more than 20 percent—the burgeoning economy would take all the well-educated workers it could get.

At this point in the short history of standards, we should pause and reflect that indeed the information economy has boomed as the nation's top leaders foresaw. Ten years later, there are jobs for all who want them, especially using computer technology. The economy could absorb many more technologically educated workers: the U.S. Immigration and Naturalization Service (INS) issues 115,000 special visas a year for computer programmers, high-technology specialists, and scientific research workers because the supply of U.S. workers in these field is inadequate.[4] The people who have left the welfare rolls with the end of generous welfare programs find that the chief obstacle to a living wage is lack of education, especially in computer technology.

As a result of that education conference in 1989, every governor endorsed six National Education Goals (later expanded to eight). Goal number 3 promoted standards development by demanding high achievement from all students in six major academic areas.[5]

YES—STANDARDS ARE FEASIBLE, DESIRABLE, AND POSSIBLE IN THE UNITED STATES!

Shortly after the establishment of the National Education Goals, a bipartisan committee was assigned to study the desirability and feasibility of national standards and assessments. The National Council on Education Standards and Testing (with the unfortunate acronym NCEST) was a thirty-two member working group widely representative of federal and state elected officials, business leaders, researchers, and teachers. Members included the heads of teachers unions as well as education's high-profile critics, Chester Finn and Lynne Cheney. It was cochaired by South Carolina's Republican governor, Carroll A. Campbell Jr., and Colorado's Democratic governor, Roy Romer.

This remarkable committee met several times during the fall of 1991 in sessions open to the public. It was charged with determining whether standards were feasible, desirable, and possible in the United States. They quickly concluded that "in the absence of well-defined and demanding standards, education in the United States has gravitated toward *de facto* national minimum expectations, with curricula focusing on low-level reading and arithmetic skills and on small amounts of factual material in other content areas."[6] They were firm in what they wanted: high national standards for all students.

The report from this council exemplified the broad bipartisan support national standards enjoyed early in the decade. The standards would be voluntary; there was no attempt to tread on state and local determination of education policy. They would be written through a far-reaching process intended to engage all stakeholders in a public conversation about what is important for students to know and be able to do. Assessments, also voluntary, would be designed so states could monitor student progress toward content standards.[7] Finally, so-called opportunity-to-learn standards would be developed to help states figure out how to deliver instruction to all students so they could meet high content standards.

Unfortunately, the consensus for standards that began the decade did not hold. Within a short time conservative Christian groups began to protest what they viewed as federal intrusion into family lives by promoting a "politically correct" curriculum. The backlash was inspired by rather feeble-minded outcomes written without public input by the Pennsylvania Department of Education. The outcry rolled across the country. School-board meetings were disrupted by angry parents who sniffed out signs of "outcome-based education" in the most innocuous propositions. Political campaigns were held hostage to the fears of this small but vocal minority. The controversy reached its fevered pitch with the release of the first draft of national history standards, which have the distinction of being officially censured by both sides of the aisle in the U.S. Senate.

But the opposition began to lose steam as states and districts published their own standards and other national documents were released to general approval. The controversial history standards were sent back to the drawing board and reemerged stronger. The public was able to see for itself that the standards weren't the threat to their values as opponents had claimed, and in fact fairly captured the academic goals parents want for their children. But while adults wasted time arguing, children languished in outdated classrooms.

WHO WROTE THESE STANDARDS?

When teachers ask this question, we frequently give a surprising answer: "*You* did." They look puzzled because they don't remember doing anything of the kind. We mean that teachers were essential partners in the development of standards. Their professional associations wrote them and asked for reviews from a wide swath of their members as well as from the broader public.

Following the report of NCEST, the U.S. Department of Education was authorized to grant funds to professional organizations to develop voluntary national standards. One group—the mathematics teachers—was way ahead of the game. The National Council of Teachers of Mathematics (NCTM) had been working on standards since the mid-1980s, when as a group they recognized the need for updating mathematics teaching in view of the coming demands for mathematically literate—"numerate"—workers. In 1989 they published their *Curriculum and Evaluation Standards for School Mathematics,* and it became the gold standard for standards writers in other subjects.[8] The NCTM received no funds from the U.S. Department of Education, but funded the entire process itself, including two cycles of review by NCTM members who were classroom teachers, curriculum specialists, mathematics professors, and teacher educators.

In the course of the next few years after the governors adopted the education goals, national standards were developed in history (1996), science (1993 and 1996), geography (1994), and the arts (1994). They all followed the draft-and-review process developed by the NCTM pioneers with the addition of public hearings. The national standards were not developed directly by the U.S. Department of Education, but by professional associations parallel to the NCTM that applied to the department for the available funds.[9] Some professional associations followed the NCTM model and produced their own standards with private funds. This resulted in social studies standards, economics standards, health and physical education standards, and two sets of science standards, one produced by the National Research Council with federal

funds, and one produced by the American Association for the Advancement of Science with their own funds.[10]

The years when national standards were first produced were heady times for U.S. education. The air was full of discussions about what the U.S. public really wanted students to know and be able to do in academic disciplines. There was hope that we would be able to define these concepts and skills—that a high school diploma would have some meaning beyond time spent in school.

As noted, discussions about the content that students should master became acrimonious, especially in history, but the movement went forward. Action on standards popped up everywhere. At the same time that the voluntary national standards were being written, a group funded by private foundations, the National Center on Education and the Economy (NCEE), was convening groups of teachers and experts to develop standards and assessments that they intended should be adopted by states and districts. The NCEE published the *New Standards Performance Standards* in 1997 in three oversize volumes: standards at grades 4, 8, and 10 in mathematics, English/language arts, science, and applied learning. Although the assessments and curriculum developed to accompany the *New Standards* have not been widely adopted, the standards themselves have been influential, especially in English/language arts. We shall refer to their elementary standards in our listing of standards in the next chapter.

We have already mentioned the National Assessment of Educational Progress (NAEP), the only nationally administered test in the United States. It acts as a dipstick into the state of U.S. education, with tests every two and four years in major subjects at grades 4, 8, and 12. At the beginning of the 1990s, under the influence of the national standards, NAEP developed what it called Frameworks for its tests in reading, writing, mathematics, science, history, geography, and the arts. These NAEP Frameworks, essentially mini-standards, distilled the national standards into usable guides for teaching. The NAEP Reading Framework, for example, made a sensible synthesis out of the opposing forces in the teaching of reading: those who believe in phonics and those who swear by whole language methods.

In those optimistic days there were even proposals under the Bush administration for a voluntary national test that would report on individual student progress toward the national standards. President Clinton picked up the banner, calling for voluntary tests for grade 3 reading and grade 8 mathematics. Groups began to design and pilot possible test items. However, the idea did not survive the Republican-led Congress in the mid-1990s. It is ironic to contemplate the failure to establish a national test in the most advanced democracy in the world, when almost every other country regards nationwide tests and examinations as routine.

The peculiar organization of U.S. education not only ended the movement toward a national test, it also precluded the adoption of national standards. Education in the United States is considered a matter for states and local education authorities, so states wanted their own standards-development processes. Although for the most part these state standards drew heavily on the national standards and on the *New Standards Performance Standards,* they were written by groups in each state, sometimes consisting mainly of state education department and state capital personnel, in other cases drawing on a wide representation of a state's teachers and citizens. By 1999 only Iowa still had no document that could be called standards.[11]

Large districts soon got into the act. Chicago actually wrote standards in 1991 and has already discarded them and formulated a second set of standards. Cities with their own standards now include Atlanta, New York, Los Angeles, Cincinnati, and El Paso, Texas. The process is still going on. Although all districts can (and in many cases, must) use state standards, local districts still feel the need to engage in the conversation about the knowledge and skills to be expected of their children. Doing so provides a sense of ownership and responsibility.

HOW CAN STANDARDS MAKE A DIFFERENCE?

Education in the United States often seems to teachers and others to be a series of fads that come and go. Fad-weary people look at standards and ask, "What is it this time?" But this is a fundamentally different movement. As we have seen from the history of standards development, the standards movement has its origins outside the education system, and the energy to sustain it is also coming from outside. Indeed, some big-city school systems—New York, San Diego, Los Angeles, Chicago—now have superintendents whose training and backgrounds are in business and government. The source of the standards and trends toward involving people outside the traditional education community indicates the pressure on the educational system for basic changes.[12] As instruments of change, the standards are serious and are here to stay.

So what do standards offer that open classrooms, constructivism, cooperative learning, or multiple intelligences don't? Standards provoke a fundamental rethinking of the system, a revision that promises to make it work finally for all students. Here are some reasons why:

1. *Coherence.* Standards provide the thread to make education coherent. All elements must be aligned—curriculum, instruction, assessments—with the standards. Needless to say, all the elements are definitely not yet aligned. An obvious example of misalignment: many states are trying to assess progress toward standards with norm-referenced tests, a logical impossibility as we shall see in chapter seven when we discuss tests and assessments. But coherence is within our grasp as it has never been before.

   Understanding what all students must learn gives a clear focus for all levels of governance, from the school board to the U.S. Department of Education, and for all personnel, from the students themselves to superintendents. For their ability to focus the crazy quilt of U.S. education, the standards are worth all the stress and pain of changing systems to meet them.

2. *Everyone can see what students should learn.* Standards work by making public expectations for all students. The fact that they are *public* does the trick. Standards lay out what all students should know and be able to do to make the system accountable as never before. Parents can take the state (or local) standards to their teacher conferences, to a principal, or to a school-board meeting—and ask what the school is doing to ensure that their children will meet that standard at the appropriate benchmark.

   Teachers have a gauge by which to measure their classroom activities. The criterion is no longer, "Will the kids enjoy this?" or "Is this appropriate for Thanksgiving, or Presidents Day?" The criterion for judging an activity now is: "Is this aligned with the standards?" Of course children should have enjoyable activities from which to learn, but the activities must be directly connected to learning.

3. *Curriculum is unrestricted.* Standards potentially free up schools to do whatever it takes to get students to standards, although few have realized that freedom so far. Because standards provide a yardstick by which to judge any program, schools can choose the program they wish, so long as it is aligned with standards and allows students to achieve them. Programs such as Success for All, Direct Instruction, Expeditionary Learning, and Core Knowledge, as well as project-based learning, approaches to instruction such as constructivism and teaching to multiple intelligences, and a host of other programs and approaches, must all be judged by their results. Similarly, standards will pronounce the final word on new governance structures such as charter schools or for-profit educational management services such as the Edison Project. If all these initiatives enable students to reach the standards and gain the skills and knowledge listed in them, then one approach or program is as good as another.

   Teachers have a new tool for judging the quality of what they are planning for their classrooms. No matter how much the teacher and the students enjoy the lesson on butterflies, if it does not require the students to read or write or otherwise move them toward standards, it has to go. So do lessons that teach only cooperation or following directions or neatness without significant content.

   Creativity is not being stifled; when school personnel understand clearly what students must know and be able to do, they can search among a wide variety of programs, approaches, and materials for curricular activities.

4. *Learning is the focus of elementary school.* Student learning is the focus of the standards movement—learning, not teaching, for success is judged by results, not by inputs. Schools are now expected to be responsible for ensuring that students learn, not just for delivering instruction. Teachers can no longer say, "I taught addition and subtraction with double digits, but they just didn't get it." Teaching is now the art of finding ways to help all children learn academic content.

   The responsibility of teachers is dramatically illustrated by new research that correlates individual teachers with student scores on standardized tests. As we shall discuss in greater detail in chapter four, evidence is now available that teaching is the single most important factor in student success. And student success means that the material has been learned, not simply delivered.

Because all students must meet the standards, the distribution of resources is being rethought. Resources include time.[13] Schools that are successful in meeting standards may offer after-school tutoring, Saturday school, or summer school to provide more opportunities to learn for children who need it. Principals are reorganizing their teaching staffs so that elementary school students get the help they need to read and write in first grade, even kindergarten.

5. *Education is now about outcomes—academic outcomes—even in elementary school.* Before the standards movement, emphasis was on regulating inputs in districts and schools—monitoring compliance with national, state, and district rules. Inputs were expected to be fairly equal, but it was accepted as normal that outcomes—the results in terms of student achievement—were going to be unequal. Some students would do well and go off to college, and some would go into the military or into jobs; some would drop out—a sad fact, but not one we could do a lot about.

Under a standards-based system of education, inputs and outcomes are reversed: outcomes must be equal—all students must meet standards—but the inputs necessary for this to happen are unequal. Some students need more time and resources, and their schools need more money to ensure that students meet standards.

An example pertinent to elementary schools in particular is the shift in Title 1, the major source of federal funds to school districts. Title 1 is intended to help schools that serve low-income students to break the pattern of poverty and low achievement. The majority of U.S. schools, mainly elementary although increasingly secondary, receive Title 1 funds. When Title 1 was reauthorized in 1994, it embodied the changes we've mentioned. It became standards-based.

In previous funding periods, Title 1, formerly called Chapter 1, was a program in which qualifying students were usually pulled out of the classroom for remedial help in reading and mathematics. Much of the money went to employ classroom aides and specialists so that Title 1 became in many cities an employment program, especially for minorities and for second-language communities. Research showed depressingly little result for the large numbers of dollars poured into Chapter 1/Title 1 in twenty-five years of its operations.[14]

But in 1994, under the influence of the standards movement, Congress made sweeping changes in the Title 1 law. It is no longer supposed to be a pull-out remedial program, but one involving whole schools and focusing on achieving standards for all students. A school should aim for all its students to meet the standards so that instruction becomes more rigorous not only for the poor students, but for the others as well.

Because the Title 1 funds include a percentage for teacher development and emphasize its importance, some school districts have reshaped their Title 1 programs to reduce the number of classroom aides and provide training in standards implementation for their teachers. One extremely poor elementary school in Colorado, where all the children are eligible for Title 1, reorganized its staff so that no classroom has more than eighteen children. Its results on tests in reading and mathematics have been so dramatic that the school now attracts visitors eager to see how it's done.

6. *Redefining "play."* The emphasis on academic learning and results is repugnant to many traditional early childhood advocates and specialists. They believe that young children should enjoy learning through play and not be burdened with letters or counting until they are in first grade—or even later.

However, children themselves don't agree. Present them with the alphabet or with any number of objects to count, and they eagerly learn, especially if they can chant them in unison! As we described in chapter one, we have been mobbed in kindergarten classes by children eager to read to us. There is no evidence that these children are overburdened by intellectual challenges—they obviously make no distinction between learning and play.

In the Crown Heights area of Brooklyn there is a preschool run by a woman in her seventies where children learn the alphabet, can count, and retell stories. Many of them can read words before they enter kindergarten. The school is private, but only because the owner could not persuade public schools that children can learn at age four and that poor inner-city children need that early stimulation more than others. After she got exasperated with officials telling her that young children need time to play and explore their world undirected by teachers, she decided that she had to go outside the system to help children. She proves the officials wrong and the children right daily.

———

The standards don't just have potential—they are already having an effect. Looking back on the changes perceptible in U.S. education since we wrote the first edition of *Smart Start*, it is clear that standards-based education is fundamentally changing schooling in the United States. In its annual report on the state of standards, *Making Standards Matter 1999,* the American Federation of Teachers reported that all states have standards except Iowa, and that forty-seven assess students and report results publicly.[15] In addition—and this is important for elementary schools—fourteen states have policies for ending social promotion. In most cases, this means that students will be unable to go to grade 5 or grade 9 unless they have passed the tests for mastery of the standards at grades 4 and 8.

As the standards movement has gathered momentum, the basis of U.S. education has shifted. Even in those states and districts where the standards are only experienced through increased emphasis on tests, they have changed the atmosphere, the value system ,and the focus. And the results: a RAND report showed that remarkable gains in mathematics achievement in the first half of the 1990s have been made in those states where standards and assessments are aligned.[16] Where standards are taken seriously and affect all parts of the system, children learn.

NOTES

1. Questions about the definitions of terms such as *content standards, performance standards,* and *rubrics* are also fired at us, but to avoid becoming too technical in our general account in this chapter, we have listed the questions and answers in Appendix B.

2. The wording is from the New York City standards, but the concepts are found in most standards documents.

3. Although under consideration, graduation criteria have not yet changed on a large scale.

4. Claiborne, "In Short Supply." The article reports that special visas are now being issued to increase the number of qualified mathematics, science, and world language teachers for Chicago public schools under the same INS program.

5. The national education goals are:

    1. All children will start school ready to learn.

    2. The high school graduation rate will increase to at least 90 percent.

    3. All students will become competent in challenging subject matter.

    4. Teachers will have the knowledge and skills they need.

    5. U.S. students will be the first in the world in mathematics and science achievement.

    6. Every adult American will be literate.

    7. Schools will be safe, disciplined, and free of drugs, guns, and alcohol.

    8. Schools will promote parental involvement and participation.

The original wording of goal number 5 included the phrase "by the year 2000."

6. National Council on Education Standards and Testing, *Raising Standards for American Education.*

7. At the time we wrote the first edition of *Smart Start,* we were so confident that national tests would be written that we made the now embarrassing statement that students would begin to take these tests in 1994.

8. That first edition of the NCTM Standards was used as the basis for the mathematics curriculum in section three of the first edition of *Smart Start.*

9. No standards in English/language arts resulted because funding for the two organizations involved, the National Council of Teachers of English (NCTE) and the International Reading Association (IRA), was withdrawn by the U.S Department of Education. The NCTE and the IRA later produced national standards with their own funds.

10. The full titles of these documents and information on obtaining them are listed in Appendix D.

11. States' need to distinguish themselves resulted in different names for standards documents: some are called curriculum frameworks, others curriculum standards, core expectations, and so forth. However, they have the same purpose as what we call standards.

12. Strengthening the influence of outsiders is the fact that the two most influential statements on reading recently have come from the National Institute of Child Health and Human Development (NICHHD) of the National Institutes of Health. The first is a statement before the U.S. Senate by G. Reid Lyon, Chief of NICHHD's Child Development and Behavior Branch, and the second is a report of the National Reading Panel (see the bibliography).

13. National Commission on Time and Learning, *Prisoners of Time,* calls for the creation of "an education system geared to the demands of a new age and a different world," 9.

14. Puma et al., *Prospects.*

15. American Federation of Teachers, *Making Standards Matter, 1999.*

16. Grissmer et al., *Improving Student Achievement.*

CHAPTER THREE

WHAT STUDENTS SHOULD KNOW AND BE ABLE TO DO BEFORE THEY LEAVE ELEMENTARY SCHOOL

NOW THAT WE have described what standards are and how they came on the scene in U.S. education, we need to see what they look like. In this chapter we explain and list standards in English/language arts, mathematics, and science, history, geography, and civics for grades 1, 4, and 6.

Why these grades? In the first edition of *Smart Start,* we laid out what twelve- year-olds, or students ending sixth grade, should know and be able to do. The advent of standards at the national, state, regional, and district levels at grades 4, 8, and 12 has made it impossible to blithely repeat that procedure. Standards are available in many states and districts at every grade level (despite our warnings and unease about them, as we explain in Appendix B). In some districts and states, fourth grade is a watershed because students who cannot pass tests in mathematics and language arts cannot proceed to fifth grade.

We have decided to list standards at three important points in elementary education: at grade 1, the point where students should be able to read; at grade 4, for the reason just mentioned; and at grade 6, the end of elementary school for most children, and the point where they should be ready for secondary education.[1] There is a much greater specificity about these standards than was possible in the first edition of *Smart Start*. In the 1990s a great deal of intellectual energy went into figuring out what students should know and be able to do, and we have taken advantage of the resulting statements. The list of knowledge and abilities in the first edition of *Smart Start* was derived from our own reading and desires for elementary learning. The list in this book has the authority of teachers, administrators, and professors who have written standards usually under the direction of a state department of education or legislature. We have synthesized the contents of the list, but we are not responsible for their origins.

The establishment of standards is an immense step forward. U.S. educators, school boards, and legislators have taken the responsibility for making clear to schools and the general public what students should know and be able to do. As we said in the previous chapter, public standards bring coherence to the entire education system.

The standards in this chapter might be called composite standards, because they will not be found exactly in this form in any national, state, or local standards documents, although pieces will be recognizable from many of these documents.[2] We have synthesized and abbreviated them, for the intention here is not to provide a working document, but to indicate what standards look like and how they guide curriculum. We want to familiarize readers with standards so that they will be encouraged to ask schools for copies of the standards they are using and feel confident that they can understand their form and content. What we list here are academic standards. We do not list performance standards, rubrics, or scoring guides.[3]

Emphasizing yet again how much the scene in U.S. education has changed, we want to point out a major difference from the first edition of *Smart Start*. In that book, we did not list literacy—reading and writing—in our recommendations for an ideal elementary school "curriculum" (as we mistakenly called it), because we believed that reading and writing belong in all classes and all disciplines. We still believe this, but poor results on the National Assessment of Educational Progress, and on every other test given to students across the states and in large cities, have made clear that literacy must be the major focus of elementary education. President Clinton declared in a 1997 speech that all students should be able to read by the third grade. President George W. Bush has pledged to emphasize early reading as well. So our list includes reading and writing, listening and speaking (important but not yet well-taught aspects of literacy), as well as literature.

The standards are not listed here. Instead we have focused on what the standards mean in elementary school and how they should be used to guide instruction. The standards documents on which we have drawn are listed in Appendix D and can be easily obtained, usually on the Internet.

ENGLISH/LANGUAGE ARTS STANDARDS FOR GRADES 1, 4, AND 6

These standards will be divided into reading, writing, listening, and speaking. There are subdivisions within some of these topics.

Overview of Reading Standards

A child who cannot read cannot advance his or her academic learning. The basic purpose of the elementary school must be to ensure that students can read. Although numeracy is immensely important, literacy is fundamental because without it, students can't understand problems in mathematics or learn any other subject.[4] G. Reid Lyon of the National Institute of Child Health and Human Development reported to the U.S. Senate that if children do not read well by age nine, three-quarters of them will continue to have difficulty throughout high school and thus will be condemned to lower achievement in all other school subjects. We saw a concrete example in the story of Andrew in chapter one.

We are not going to take sides in the "reading wars" that have raged across U.S. education for at least twenty years. Neither phonics instruction nor whole language will produce readers by themselves. Recent work, especially that undertaken by the National Institute of Child Health and Human Development, makes clear that learning to read requires understanding of the print-sound code in English, called phonemic awareness; learning strategies to comprehend what is read; vocabulary development; and constant practice, in the form of hearing books read, reading books with assistance, and reading alone. Above all, students learn to read successfully if they have well-trained teachers who understand that reading is a complicated skill dependent on many factors.

But no matter how skilled teachers are, learning to read in this century presents difficulties not faced by previous generations. Before television came to every home (a diminishing proportion of people now remember such a time), the world was accessed through books. Now the world seems open to children on the TV screen or even on the small computer screen. Because children are unaware of the differences in depth between television and books, reading can seem like an enormous effort to gain rather less information than can be absorbed by watching, which takes little skill beyond keeping your eyes open.

Motivation for reading is therefore a serious issue for this generation of students and teachers. To be persuaded to make the investment in time and energy, children have to be convinced that they will gain more, both long-term and short-term, if they learn to read early and well. Long-term benefits include training for thinking deeply about the complexities facing inhabitants of this millennium, but will be hard to convey to children without clear and present proof. Short-term benefits include the pleasures of the imagination, particularly as embodied in the Harry Potter books. They have made reading socially acceptable among upper elementary students, and astute librarians have seized the moment to introduce readers to other authors while they wait for the next Harry Potter novel.

One way to convince children that reading is worthwhile is simply to point out that the Internet and World Wide Web require reading. In fact, early introduction to the computer screen may force alphabetic awareness on children through the keyboard, provided it isn't limited to icons.

In short, there is no easy solution to the problem of motivation. It is important, however, to understand that children today may be having more difficulty learning to read than those of earlier generations because of the enormous competition for their attention among school, television, the Internet, advertising, popular music, and cell phones.

The task of teaching all children to read today is further complicated by the swelling enrollments of children whose primary language is not English. Teaching children with limited English proficiency (LEP students, as they're called) is subject to its own brand of reading war: should they be completely immersed in English-only classrooms at school, or taught in their native language while they ease into English? Emotions in the debate run high while the evidence for both approaches is mixed. Which approach works best seems to depend on the individual child's circumstances. Clearly, a newly arrived twelve-year-old who lacks formal education in any language presents different educational challenges than a five-year-old who may speak another language at home but has been in this country since birth. Children in the latter group seem to adapt quickly to a predominantly English curriculum (although even a few words by the teacher in the child's native language seem to have a positive effect); the former group needs supports of many kinds. Regardless of the methodology used, the expectation that all students will eventually meet English standards must remain constant.

Reading Standards, Grade 1

The bottom line for reading is that children should be able to read by the end of first grade and be skilled readers by the end of third grade. In order to make clear what this means, the following standards are divided into three areas: phonemic awareness, comprehension, and reading experience. It is important to remember that these are standards for first grade. Standards for kindergarten precede them, so that these standards build on them—first grade is not the first time students will have sounded out phonemes or read short stories.

1. *Phonemic awareness.* By the end of first grade children should have essentially mastered the elements of the print-sound code; that is, they should be able to sound out regularly spelled one- and two-syllable words and be able to use rhyming to make new words, including blends of consonants like *br* and *cr* and digraphs, blends of two consonants making a totally different sound, like *th* and *ch*.

    They should also be able to recognize about 150 high-frequency words as they read them. English is rich in words that really can't be phonetically sounded out—the most obvious example being one. A first-grader should be able to recognize common prepositions, connectives, and question words on sight.

2.   *Comprehension.* Students should read with accuracy and fluency—that is, with sufficient speed to understand the meaning of the material they are reading. They should be able to use punctuation as indicators of meaning. They should be able to correct themselves when they misread or mistake a word, relying on both phonemic awareness and the meaning of the story.

3.   *Reading experience.* Reading experiences for young children should be of four kinds: independent reading, assisted reading, being read to, and discussing books. And there should be lots of all four experiences.

First-graders should read (independently or with help) *at least four books a day* and should hear another four books (or extracts) read to them each day. They must develop the habit of reading in order to command the vocabulary and volume of words they will need for middle and high school work—not to mention for ordinary life.

In addition, first-graders should experience *discussion* of what they read. In Lauren Resnick's principles of learning, this discussion is called accountable talk.[5] In talking about the books they have just read, children look for evidence in the text to support their opinions, and they listen to each other and build on points made by their fellow students.

Obviously, books for reading aloud to children can be more difficult than those books children need help reading, and in turn those are more difficult than books children can read independently. Books for independent reading have been "leveled" by experts with letters identifying the levels: Level A is the simplest level, for kindergarten or even preschool. First-graders are expected to read Level I books independently.[6] Here are some of these books as listed in *Reading and Writing Grade by Grade: Primary Literacy Standards for Kindergarten Through Third Grade,* written by the New Standards Primary Literacy Committee:

The Hole in Harry's Pocket (D. C. Heath and Co.,
  Little Readers)
Worms for Breakfast (Houghton Mifflin, Little Readers)
Jack and the Beanstalk (Rigby, Literacy 2000)
Ants (Wright Group, Sunshine Science Series)

Note that the last book is not a story, but a book of information about ants, intended as early science instruction. This is important: students should read all kinds of text, not just fiction, because they need to begin distinguishing how to read different kinds of material—the suspension of disbelief for fiction, for example; the sequential presentation of information in a history text; and the movement from general to specific in science texts.

Reading Standards, Grade 4

Three years on, students should be past the stage of learning to read—they should now be well into reading to learn. By the end of fourth grade, students should:

- have read at least twenty-five books (in general, the length of a typical "chapter" book) during the school year,

- have read at least four books on one subject, or by one author,

- be able to read aloud books they know well fluently and accurately, and

- be reading silently and independently—a lot.

In addition, they should be able to participate in accountable talk about their reading, showing evidence of understanding what they have read and relating new information to previous knowledge and personal experience.

They should be able to write about what they read, keeping records of the twenty-five books and four books of concentration, and they should be using computer catalogs to help them find books and information about their reading.

As for what they should read, an excellent suggested list is contained in *New Standards Performance Standards, Volume 1: Elementary School,* page 23. These examples from that list give the flavor of books that fourth-graders should have read:

Fiction
Antoine de Saint Exupery, *The Little Prince*
Faith Ringgold, *Tar Beach*
Beverly Cleary, *Ramona and Her Father*
Roald Dahl, *James and the Giant Peach*
Kenneth Grahame, *The Wind in the Willows*
E. B. White, *Charlotte's Web*
Mary Norton et al., *The Borrowers*
Chris Van Allsburg, *Jumanji*

Nonfiction
Vivian Sheldon Epstein, *History of Women in Science for Young People*
Eric Politi, *Song of the Swallows*
Helen Roney Sattler, *Dinosaurs of North America*

Poetry
Edward Blishen and Brian Wildsmith, *Oxford Book of Poetry for Children*
Arnold Lobel, ed., *The Random House Book of Mother Goose*
Shel Silverstein, *Where the Sidewalk Ends*

**Reading Standards,
Grade 6**

By the end of elementary school, students should be able to read so well that they can routinely read *USA Today* and its editorials, paraphrase the editorials, and respond to their arguments. We choose *USA Today* because it is sold throughout the United States and therefore provides a standard available to all parts of the country.

Students should have read at least twenty-five books a year, and at least four on one subject or by one author. Clearly these books will be more difficult in terms of vocabulary, complexity of ideas, and sophistication of style than those read at fourth grade.

Sixth grade is a good time to check that students have a solid bedrock of experience with the myths and legends that underlie the literature they will be expected to read in middle and high school. Here is a suggested list—not exhaustive, but exemplifying the rich well of stories that students will need as background for future reading:

Aesop's fables
Homer's *Odyssey* and Greek myths and legends
"Anansi the Spider"—an Ashanti tale
Grimms' fairy tales
Norse myths
Arthurian legends
Sir Gawaine and the Green Knight
Beowulf
Legends and folktales of Vietnam
"The Crane Wife" and other Japanese folktales
"Bo Rabbit Smart for True"—Gullah folktales
"Arrow to the Sun" and other American Indian folktales
Tales from the Arabian Nights
"Baba Yaga" and other Russian folktales
"Zlateh the Goat" and other Jewish folktales

In addition, sixth-graders should have heard or read for themselves stories from the Bible treated as literature. We are by no means recommending one religion (in this case, three—Islam, Judaism, and Christianity) over another, but suggesting that twelve- year-olds should be able to recognize the great archetypal stories contained in the Bible. Much of later literature—emerging postcolonial literatures in Africa, Australia, South America, and Asia, as well as European and American classics—refers to biblical stories. Not to know those stories is to be deprived of access to literary meanings. The stories of Noah; of Adam and Eve; of Joseph and his brothers; of Samson, Delilah, and the Philistines; of Job; of Daniel in the lions' den; and even of Jesus Christ's birth and death are all part of the world's heritage. The English language itself is permeated with references—"the serpent in the garden", "the patience of Job", "a Judas"—that are opaque without at least knowing how they originate in the Bible.

And so also with the stories of Shakespeare's plays. We know of a second-grade teacher in Los Angeles who acquaints her students with *Romeo and Juliet,* even though they are predominantly English-language learners. She tells them the story, and then has them memorize important lines and present scenes to their classmates. Shakespeare's major plays (*Hamlet, Othello, Macbeth, A Midsummer Night's Dream, Julius Caesar,* for example) have almost the same stature as biblical stories in their influence on subsequent literature. Students need to know about them so that they can fully participate in world culture. Elementary students do not need to study complete plays, something they should do in high school, but the stories should be familiar to them.

At the end of sixth grade, then, students should have a solid foundation in place for their future reading. They have read widely among the myths and legends of the world and are ready for the challenge of sophisticated literature. They are also equipped to read in all the academic disciplines, including mathematics. They can read and dissect a political argument in a popular newspaper. Through continued accountable talk they can discuss what they have read in a logical conversation.

Writing Standards, Grade 1

As with reading, it should be remembered that these standards are for first grade—standards for writing in kindergarten have preceded them. Kindergartners have been writing on their own (sometimes with highly imaginative spellings!) since they began, so first-graders are building on that experience. The writing standards are divided into three parts.

1. *The writing process.* Students write every day in school, work with their classmates to read and revise drafts, and produce at least ten pieces each year that have been revised, edited, and prepared for "publication," on a word processor if possible.

    The writing process as a teaching tool was developed by the Bay Area Writing Project and its clones, including the National Writing Project, during the 1980s. It is now universally taught as a way for students to approach an empty sheet of paper. The process begins with brainstorming and visual aids, such as concept mapping, in which a major idea is written in the center of a page and other ideas are branched off it.

From visual aids such as these the student writes a rough draft. This is read by others—either the teacher or other students—who make suggestions for revision. After a second draft and another reading, the piece must be edited for correctness in grammar, spelling, punctuation, and usage.[7] Then it is "published" by being pinned up in the classroom or the school's corridors, or perhaps preserved in a portfolio for end-of-year assessment of progress.

The writing process emphasizes the essential features of writing in the right order: content and meaning first, editing and correctness last. That is its great contribution to the teaching of writing. Until the Writing Project developed the writing process, teachers taught writing by beginning with grammar and focusing on mechanics, thus dampening any freedom in developing ideas because students were frightened to make mistakes.

However, a caution is in order: the writing process, particularly at the elementary level, can become an end in itself. To complete the writing process does not guarantee good writing. It is essentially a tool for students to use, but they should be able to use those parts of it they need and discard others. There are occasions—and even professional writers, who are compulsive revisers of their work, acknowledge this—when the first draft is the best one.

The writing process is not, strictly speaking, a standard, but a curricular device to enable students to write. Standards describe what students must be able to do, not how they must do it, as we said earlier. But the writing process is so widely accepted and is so important to teachers that it appears in many state standards and even in the *New Standards Performance Standards.*

2. *Writing in different genres.* By the end of first grade students should be able to write:

- narratives, or stories,

- informational reports,

- responses to literature, in the form of either imitation or evaluation of what they have read.

The reading standards require students to read material other than stories—factual material about science or history, or even mathematical problems. Similarly, the writing standards require students to know the different approaches, vocabularies, and styles for writing reports, instructions, and responses to literature.

This is more important than it might seem. Elementary school has traditionally been the place for children to read and write stories and to give free rein to their imaginations, all in the vein of the romantic view of childhood as a time of innocence and distance from harsh realities. But most writing in the world is not fiction, and most of the writing these students will do will not be fiction—it will be reports, memos, instructions, proposals, e-mail exchanges. Far from protecting them in a fictional world, we are doing students a service by teaching them the genres that engage them in reality.

Furthermore, as the early literacy expert Sally Hampton points out, "Fiction is a demanding form for even the most sophisticated writers, so no one should be surprised when primary students have problems writing fiction."[8] The problems are frequently masked by the adult response, "How cute!"

Nonfiction genres are actually easier to teach than fiction. Omissions and faults in sequencing in reports and instructions can be pointed out and can be fixed. In responses to literature, thinking skills are enhanced by asking for answers to the questions: "Why do you like this?" and "Why don't you like this?"

Early introduction to nonfiction genres means that from the beginning students understand that *the key to success in writing is writing for a purpose to a specific audience.* Young children can understand the differences in speaking style between speaking to their friends on the playground and speaking to the teacher, or asking their parents for something they want. Those insights can be translated into writing, along with the vocabulary and style choices made necessary by different readers and purposes in writing.

The standards lay out the need for experience in all four genres so children will get their chance to write stories. They just won't be the only things these students will write in first grade.

3. *Mechanics, usage, grammar, and spelling (MUGS).* First-graders are still using "invented" spelling, and their idea of capitalization is often to play with it by writing some words in all capitals. However, by the end of first grade they should:

- spell well enough so that another child or adult could understand the meaning,

- spell familiar words and word endings correctly,

- use words from their reading and from their spoken vocabulary, and

- use capitalization and punctuation accurately.

They should be a little adventurous in using words they haven't used before and playing with punctuation such as exclamation points and question marks, especially in imitation of their favorite authors.

Writing Standards, Grade 4

Writing standards do not change fundamentally throughout the grades. Rather, the subjects on which students write increase in complexity and intellectual challenge, and the expectations for correct use of language conventions increase in rigor.

1. *The writing process.* Students continue to use the writing process and to prepare for "publication" a polished piece of writing at least once a month.

2. *Writing in different genres.* Students should now be comfortable with the four kinds of writing expected at first grade, but now they add another: summary. This is a vital writing technique that, if mastered well at fourth grade, will go a long way to ensuring success in college and in a career. Summary combines good reading with succinct and clear writing. It must be differentiated from retelling a narrative, a distinction that will be made with the help of accountable talk, which focuses on the ideas and evidence supporting them in the text. Summary requires students to be able to identify the main idea or theme. The time spent learning how to identify the main idea will be repaid like compound interest if it is acquired at fourth grade. Students will not need classes in "thinking skills" if they can summarize well, either orally or in writing.

3. *Mechanics, usage, grammar, and spelling (MUGS).* Not only should students know and use all the basic conventions of English grammar, usage, and spelling, they should also know how to edit and correct their finished work using spell-check programs and dictionaries. By the end of fourth grade there should essentially be no major mistakes in MUGS.

Writing Standards, Grade 6

By the end of sixth grade, when students are ready to move into the middle grades, they should be fully in command of writing either by hand or on a word processor. They should be able to use the writing process but recognize that some situations make it impossible: when writing for a test or assessment, the time allotted usually permits only one draft.[9]

Students should also show some experimentation in vocabulary and style, along with a sophisticated awareness of audience and purpose when writing. There should be no errors in MUGS.

Students should be able to write in at least the following genres at the end of sixth grade:

- summary,

- narrative,

- persuasive,

- reports of information and explanations, including those expected in history, science, and mathematics,

- instructions ("how to"),

- response to literature, which includes critical skills such as identifying themes in several books, characterizing the differences among genres, understanding author's point of view, examining the reasons for characters' actions and distinguishing fully drawn characters from stereotypes, and drawing conclusions about contexts, events, characters, and settings.

**Listening and
Speaking Standards,
Grade 1**

Listening and speaking have been taught informally for many years, but their importance to success both in school and in the world of work is becoming recognized so that formal expectations are now widespread. Speaking is not yet assessed much outside the classroom, but a few tests do include listening, in the form of either audiotapes or structured reading by the teacher.

At first grade, listening and speaking skills resemble accountable talk. Students can listen attentively and respond to what has been said, whether by an adult or another student. First-graders can be clearly understood, not only in the presentation of their ideas, but also because they use proper phrasing, pitch, and modulation.

Students can make brief prepared reports about a topic to their classmates, keeping to a specified amount of time. There may be mistakes in grammar and sentence structure, but the meaning will be clear.

**Listening and
Speaking Standards,
Grade 4**

After three more years of experience with guided speech and structured presentations, students should be able to converse with both adults and fellow students to obtain information, ask questions, provide directions, and make supported comments on others' ideas.

They should also be able to summarize orally what they have heard; for example, a short narrative or an explanation given by the teacher.

In addition to being able to use speech themselves, students should now be able to make reasoned critiques of what they hear, either in the classroom or through the public media.

Listening and Speaking Standards, Grade 6

At the end of elementary school, students should be able to use listening and speaking as a tool in their learning and in their social interactions. They should be able to use oral skills politically, in the sense that they can call and hold meetings and mount campaigns for class offices.

They will make presentations in all subject areas of about five or seven minutes' length, using notes as necessary and visual aids. They will begin the presentation with a statement of the main idea or purpose; support it with details, examples, and reasons; and then conclude with a summary of the main points.

They will be discerning listeners, able to help others with useful critical commentaries and able to evaluate what they hear through the media.

MATHEMATICS, STANDARDS FOR GRADES 1, 4, AND 6

In literacy there was an enormous controversy over the teaching of phonics as opposed to whole language; similarly, in mathematics the 1990s have seen the "math wars," which pitch those who advocate problem solving and understanding processes against those who advocate mastery of algorithms. Again, we are not going to get into that fight or take sides: we believe that elementary students must know the multiplication tables and also be able to solve multistep problems and explain their reasoning in writing.

We also believe that part of mathematics in elementary school is learning not only how to use a calculator, but also when that use is appropriate. There is no point in trying to ban calculators from any grade—kindergartners use big ones where the pads are large enough for them to hit the numbers using their still-developing small-muscle skills. On the other hand, using calculators does not exempt students from learning the multiplication tables or being able to estimate when their answer is likely to be right. Like all forms of technology, from the pencil to the voice-recognition computer, calculators are tools. It is the job of schools to teach students to use them for more efficient learning.

Above all, elementary school should produce students who like mathematics, are not afraid of it, are confident in their abilities, and understand how important it is for their futures—whether they will study engineering in college or become historians or writers. Mathematics is extending its domain in our lives. More and more decisions that used to be regarded as matters of judgment are now informed by data and calculation. Mathematics is used to make economic and political decisions as well as personal decisions such as investing and purchasing. Students should expect that they will be able to use mathematics as a tool to assist them in every part of their lives, from paying for college to voting.

The sophistication of the mathematical knowledge and skills expected at early grades may be a surprise. It shouldn't be. Algebra has its roots in patterns, which begin in kindergarten, and statistics and probability are easily understood in terms of spinners and coin tossing. It is the *continuity* of mathematics that has been freshly recognized: the progression from simple operations to the most sophisticated mathematics enabling space exploration is only a series of sequential steps. Mathematics in elementary school should feel like the first step in an exciting journey.

Here we have divided mathematics into five divisions: arithmetic and numbers; geometry and measurement; algebra and functions; statistics and probability; and problem solving and communication.

Mathematics Standards, Grade 1

1. *Arithmetic and numbers.* Students should be able to add two and three numbers that add up to ten; count forward and backward to ten; know the difference between odd and even numbers; use money to practice decimals; recognize a half, a third, and a quarter and what they mean; and be able to use the symbols for *less than*, *greater than*, and *equal to*.

2. *Geometry and measurement.* Students can measure length and weight using the U.S. and the metric system; use and understand

the difference between Fahrenheit and Celsius thermometers; and identify shapes such as squares, rectangles, triangles, and circles.

3. *Algebra and functions.* Students can recognize and extend simple patterns, using shapes, objects, and numbers; and classify using two characteristics, such as color and shape.

4. *Statistics and probability.* Students should be able to collect data and display their results on simple graphs; understand and predict what happens when a coin is tossed; and solve problems such as: "How many different pairs of numbers add up to ten?"

5. *Problem solving and communication.* Students can explain their answers to simple problems, orally and in writing; they can also write simple word problems. They show an ability to approach a problem and reason it out rather than ask immediately whether they add or subtract.

Mathematics Standards, Grade 4

1. *Arithmetic and numbers.* Students should be using all the arithmetical operations with ease—addition, subtraction, multiplication, and division, including knowing the multiplication tables; know about "special" numbers, such as primes, squares, and multiples; be able to use simple fractions and percents; and use rounding and estimation in arriving at answers.

2. *Geometry and measurement.* Students should be able to draw simple maps with coordinates; estimate and measure the size of figures and objects in the real world (i.e., not with a ruler, but with comparisons to known lengths, such as their own height, size of hand or foot, etc.); differentiate and draw perimeter, area, circumference, and volume; and model lines of symmetry.

3. *Algebra and functions.* Students will be able to describe and extend repeating and growing patterns of numbers; use symbols to stand for numbers or objects; and thus begin to understand what is meant by a *variable*.

4. *Statistics and probability*. Students understand what *sampling* means by gathering data about a group through a statistical sample; find the average, median, mode, and range of a set of numbers; combine and arrange a group of objects; and show data in different kinds of graphs—histograms, pie charts, line graphs.

5. *Problem solving and communication*. Students create, analyze, and solve their own word problems; have several approaches to problem solving at their fingertips, such as drawing diagrams, modeling, and analogizing to previous problems; can explain their problem-solving process and answers orally and in writing; and have accurate mathematical vocabularies (words such as *horizontal, vertical, divisor, dividend, quotient, product, numerator, denominator, mean, median, mode,* and *range*).

Mathematics Standards, Grade 6

1. *Arithmetic and numbers*. Students at the sixth grade and ready to go into middle school or junior high school should thoroughly understand multiples of ten up to billions and should be able to round off to the nearest 10,000; they should understand the number line, with positive and negative numbers; use all arithmetical operations on fractions and decimals; and be able to use "special" numbers and the concepts of common divisors and multiples.

2. *Geometry and measurement*. Students ready for secondary education should know the value of π and be able to use it to find the circumference and area of circles; draw to scale; find the area and perimeter of regular polygons; find the volume of regular prisms; and understand the concept of parallel and perpendicular lines.

3. *Algebra and functions*. Students ready for the formal study of algebra should understand ratio and proportion; use fractional

notation for ratios; understand the correct order of operations in an algebraic expression; and use ordered pairs of numbers to locate points on a grid and to construct figures.

4.   *Statistics and probability.* Students should be able to conduct and predict the outcomes of experiments; collect data to describe an experiment; and use the average or mean to interpret data.

5.   *Problem solving and communication.* Students should be able to create, analyze, and solve problems in all the areas of mathematics studied in elementary school; solve multistep problems and explain their process and results in writing; work in groups with other students on problems; and use mathematical terms with ease in describing how mathematics is used in everyday life.

As we said earlier, the overall mathematics standard for elementary school is the attainment of mathematical knowledge and skills so that the students can begin algebra in junior high or middle school.

SCIENCE STANDARDS FOR GRADES 1, 4, AND 6

Science is probably more clearly divided into knowledge and skills than other disciplines. We will list expected knowledge in life, physical, and earth and space science, but a child who left elementary school thinking that science is facts in textbooks (or even hamsters in cages in the corner of the classroom) would have missed the point. To make sure that this does not happen, and that students experience the pleasures of discovery, the science standards emphasize inquiry, observation, and hypothesis formation.

Because of this emphasis, science in elementary school can be taught simultaneously with mathematics and with visual art. Doubling mathematics and science seems inherently reasonable because much of science is data collection and display. But visual art? Close observation is the common element. Insight into the nature of both art and science will result from training exact observing skills: ask students to draw exactly what they see in a seedling emerging from the earth, not what they expect to see, for example. This training is another example of how "thinking skills" can be developed within a subject and need not be taught separately.

Although science in elementary school should develop skills needed for biology, chemistry, and physics in secondary school, it should perhaps develop skills for life even more. The habit of questioning, of wondering why, of trying out explanations and testing them is fundamental to understanding the world and how it works.

Science Standards, Grade 1

1. *Scientific processes.* Students know by the end of first grade what it means to observe something carefully. They can draw what they see and explain it. They count and measure to acquire data about simple experiments. They can formulate simple hypotheses about "what will happen" and report on what did happen.

2. *Scientific knowledge.* Students know the basic properties of common materials such as rocks; know the different forms of water and how they change; recognize the effects of light, heat, and magnetism; and know the life cycle of plants and animals and how they depend on their environment for food.

    They communicate their knowledge and discoveries through drawing, writing, and the display of data in bar graphs.

Science Standards, Grade 4

1. *Scientific processes.* Students can use the tools and technologies of science (rulers, computers, balances, thermometers, magnifiers, microscopes) to collect data, make observations, and analyze results. They perform at least one full investigation during the school year, such as an experiment or a systematic observation. They write up the results using graphs and diagrams, on computers where possible.

2. *Scientific knowledge.* Students know the difference between stars and planets and the relation between the Earth, and the sun and

moon; know that living things are made up of cells with different functions; know that fossils are evidence of extinction; and understand how electricity flows through a circuit.

Science Standards, Grade 6

1. *Scientific processes.* Students now understand the difference between description and explanation and recognize accurately what constitutes evidence. They understand that scientists often repeat experiments and that results can vary within a range. They are able to evaluate the design of experiments. They conduct an experiment or investigation and communicate the results using computer graphics.

2. *Scientific knowledge.* Students go into middle or junior high school with a large amount of knowledge about life and physical science and earth and space science, ready for the precision and extension of language that will come in secondary school. They know about mass and volume and are ready to learn about density. They know the properties of materials and are ready to learn the chemical elements. They know about fossils and are ready to understand evolution. They know about heat and light and are ready to learn energy flow through various systems.

Above all, they know that science makes them think—and that thinking is intensely pleasurable and rewarding.

HISTORY, GEOGRAPHY, AND CIVICS STANDARDS FOR GRADES 1, 4, AND 6

For many people, we are talking about "social studies" here. That's the name by which the subject is known in many elementary schools. However, we would like to approach it through three disciplines that have national standards and a corresponding history of intellectual inquiry: history and geography are both departments on postsecondary campuses, and civics becomes the study of constitutional law at that level. Social studies does not enjoy that legitimacy and furthermore can deteriorate into condescending descriptions of community institutions without

a core of objective inquiry. In some elementary schools, social studies becomes little more than social adjustment or conflict resolution.[10]

The study of history should take students out of their own personal worlds into a past filled with exciting narratives and fascinating people. No child should leave elementary school without being able to outline U.S. history and the major events of world history. Geography should explain many of those events, especially the reasons for the early development of civilizations in the Middle East; the major arteries of commerce such as the Silk Road and the circumnavigations of the globe during the Renaissance; and the westward expansion of the United States. Students should understand that weather moves from west to east and why the ocean currents affect climate. Civics should enable students to understand the levels of government, the balance of powers, and the duties of a citizen in the United States.

The national standards for history, geography, and civics are treated similarly (and therefore so are the state and local standards which follow the national standards closely) in that they are divided into various aspects of their complex subjects. History has five standards for historical thinking and eight for historical knowledge, geography has eighteen standards divided (unevenly) into six topics, and civics has twenty-nine standards across five topics. In some cases, history and civics standards do not apply to grades 1 and 4, and occasionally not to grade 6 either. To list them all would provide less insight than summaries of what should be expected at each grade level. So we provide summaries here.

History Standards, Grade 1

The important historical thinking skills at all levels are the ability to understand chronology; to distinguish between primary and secondary sources; and the need to be skeptical and cautious about historical information, balancing differing accounts against each other in order to arrive at a defensible consensus. At first grade, students make a significant beginning on these skills, even understanding primary sources through interviews with older people in their families and communities.

Students at the end of first grade can construct simple timelines, using pictures or artifacts, about their own family history or their own lives. They know stories about the Pilgrims, George Washington and Abraham

Lincoln, Harriet Tubman and Martin Luther King Jr., and how they changed the course of U.S. history. They can explain the history of major holidays celebrated by groups in their communities. They can ask questions that show they are conscious of differences in historical accounts: how did Europeans view the voyage of Christopher Columbus? How did the Native American peoples view the same encounter? Students' knowledge is conveyed in written reports and drawings.

**History Standards,
Grade 4**

Students use their developing historical thinking skills to establish the major events of the history of their own state, including interactions with native populations, migrations of people into the state and what caused them, and the economic status of different ethnic groups. They know the major shape of U.S. history, including the American Revolution, the Civil War, and the World Wars, although their knowledge is mainly in terms of the people involved. They can explain all the patriotic holidays and relate them to their originating events. They can describe the features of major world civilizations in terms of people's lives, and they can explain the voyages of discovery and what motivated them. They report their knowledge in writing.

**History Standards,
Grade 6**

By the time students are ready to leave elementary school for middle or junior high school, they can bring historical skills to bear on a wide range of topics in U.S. and world history. They know the general shape of events from pre-Columbian civilizations to the present. They can reconstruct the chronology of critical events leading to the Revolutionary and Civil Wars; understand different perspectives on these events; and recognize the difference between primary and secondary sources. They realize that there are different points of view about the past, and no single view is necessarily right or wrong. In world history, they know what the world looked like in terms of population density at major turning points; where and why civilizations developed and spread; and the development of the great religions of the world and their effect on political and social events.

They should know the extent of the Roman Empire and the reasons for its domination of the Western world and its legacy to the present, and the development of the civilizations of Egypt, India, China, and Japan. They analyze and report on their knowledge in written reports, including illustrations and maps acquired from the Internet.

**Geography Standards,
Grade 1**

Students can map their journey from home to school, drawing major landmarks; know the directions of the compass in relation to their school and home; know the climate of their community and how it is determined by its location; understand how human activity—industry and automobile exhaust—cause pollution; and can show on a map where the major events of U.S. history took place. They convey their learning in maps, drawings, and written reports.

**Geography Standards,
Grade 4**

Students can use all the means of representing the physical aspects of the world, including satellite images. They can draw a map of the world showing the correct relationships between the continents. They know the geographic characteristics of their own state, and how these have affected where people live. They can also explain how the characteristics of certain states affected the events of U.S. history. In a parallel to world history, they can show the Silk Road and the major explorations on a map and explain the reasons why those routes were taken. They write about their knowledge in reports illustrated with maps, on computers where possible.

**Geography Standards,
Grade 6**

By the end of elementary school, students understand the difference between different projections of the globe on maps. They can use the concept of regions to explain geographic and climatic features and how they affect population, especially the development of major centers of civilization. They can explain major migrations in terms of contextual features and barriers. They use their geographic knowledge to analyze history and their own everyday experiences. They write to report results of analyses, draw maps, and enhance their writing with illustrations and graphics made on computers and acquired from the Internet.

Civics Standards,
Grade 1

Students understand the concept of authority within their home, school, and community; recognize that authority is specific and limited; and understand that justice and fairness are the same thing. They write about their knowledge in stories and reports.

Civics Standards,
Grade 4

Students know the fundamental principles of U.S. democracy as expressed in the Declaration of Independence, the Constitution, and the Bill of Rights, and how these documents define authority. They can distinguish among the levels of government (national, state, and local) and know who their congressional representatives are. They understand the organization of their own state government and what its duties and responsibilities are. They write about their knowledge in reports and in letters to the appropriate local and state officials.

Civics Standards,
Grade 6

Students leaving elementary school have the basic knowledge needed to understand their duties and responsibilities as U.S. citizens: they know how the government is structured and how the justice system works. They know how the U.S. Constitution differs from constitutions in other countries and understand the concept of limited government. They use their knowledge of different forms of government to understand developments in U.S. and world history. They can write analyses and comparisons of different systems of government.

At the end of elementary school, students will have learned from their work in history, geography, and civics how the social and political worlds have developed in their physical context. They should have a firm sense of their place in space and time and of what they owe both to the past and to the future as citizens of the world.

PULLING THE
STANDARDS TOGETHER

As we said earlier, these summaries are merely tastes of the standards to give an idea of how statements of expectations at three stages in elementary school are structured. Even from these summary statements it is clear that students are expected to move to the next stage of their education with a strong basis of skills and knowledge.

They should be both readers and writers, with a bedrock of experience in reading appropriate classics and contemporary books and be able to write several genres of communication without errors in language conventions. They should be ready for algebra, but also sophisticated in their understanding of statistics and probability. They should understand the phenomena of the natural and physical world and be eager to ask questions about everything from the stars to a computer chip. And they should enjoy knowing the great stories of history, gaining confidence from knowing their own origins and their place in the democracy they inhabit.

In short, sixth-graders, twelve years old, are ready for the work of secondary school, secure in a foundation of skills and knowledge that puts no limits on their futures.

NOTES

1. We are aware that districts vary in their configuration of schools: many elementary schools consist of pre-K through grade 5; others go to grade 6. Some do neither, but divide all their schools into pre-K through grade 8, and high school. However, even those with different definitions of elementary and secondary education usually acknowledge a division between grade 6 and grade 7. Instruction becomes departmentalized and students no longer stay in the same classroom with the same teacher for all their subjects.

2. The standards documents we used are listed in Appendix D, along with two syntheses of standards that we drew on: Council for Basic Education *Standards for Excellence in Education*, and Kendall and Marzano *Content Knowledge*, from the Mid-Continent Regional Education Laboratory.

3. See Appendix B for definitions of terms.

4. Research into failure in mathematics shows that much of the problem lies in the fact that the students can't read the questions and understand what mathematical operation is needed.

5. The eight principles of learning guide professional development in Learning Institutes, designed and taught by Lauren Resnick of the New Standards Project and the Learning Research and Development Center at the University of Pittsburgh. The eight principles are: organize for effort; clear expectations; recognition of accomplishment; fair and credible evaluations; academic rigor in a thinking curriculum; accountable talk; socializing intelligence; and learning as apprenticeship.

6. Many publishers of children's books provide helpful guidance on their book jackets as to the approximate reading level of the text. In addition, book stores often organize their shelves to make it easier to distinguish a grade 1 story book (beginning) from a grade 3 "chapter" book (intermediate), for example.

7. A colleague at the Education Trust invented a mnemonic for these indispensable features: MUGS, for mechanics, usage, grammar, and spelling.

8. New Standards Primary Literacy Committee, *Reading and Writing Grade by Grade*, 35.

9. Some state assessments, notably the Maryland School Performance Assessment Program, allow students to work at a piece of writing over a few days so they can follow the steps of the writing process if they wish.

10. History standards were written under the auspices of the U.S. Department of Education by the National Center for History in the Schools at UCLA, with the usual input and review by teachers. However, they were attacked viciously when published and even condemned in the U.S. Senate. A revised edition met with less criticism, but the damage had been done. Geography standards were developed by the National Geographic Society, using their own funds. The national civics standards were developed with U.S. Department of Education funds by the Center for Civic Education. The National Council for the Social Studies developed and published standards at its own expense, but they suffer not only from a vague definition of their subject but also from frequent departures from describing standards (the WHAT of schooling) into prescriptions for curriculum (the HOW).

CHAPTER FOUR

WHY WE
AREN'T
THERE YET

W E NOW KNOW what students must learn in elementary
school if they are to escape Andrew's fate and move toward a successful adult life. Before the transition to a
standards-based education system can be complete, districts and their communities must make a wholesale change in thinking.
This chapter will point to some of the assumptions that mire elementary
education in outdated practices and also to insights that show the way to
redesigning instruction.

In the first edition of *Smart Start* we defined four guiding principles
that are essential to providing a first-class education to all students. Nine
years later, we still think they're pretty good. We present them again with
some minor modification to acknowledge how education reform has
progressed, or in some cases regressed, over the decade.

An effective elementary program will be guided by these principles:

1. All children can learn.

2. All children know something.

3.   Teachers are central to students' learning.

4.   Instruction should be balanced.

A discussion of each of these principles follows.

1. ALL CHILDREN CAN LEARN

Everyone says it. In fact, "All children can learn" is stated so often it risks becoming another banality along the lines of "Have a nice day." But the record shows that if educators believe that all children can learn, they surely do not believe they can learn the same things.

Practices such as tracking and ability grouping abound in elementary schools, despite the wary scrutiny they now receive from a wide array of advocates and watchdogs, including the Office of Civil Rights in the U.S. Department of Education. At the extreme academic ends, politically popular "gifted and talented" programs flourish unthreatened by shrinking school budgets, and special education programs can't hire enough teachers for their ever-expanding enrollments. The majority of children who are caught in between face uncertain prospects. They may either find excitement and academic challenge in the classroom, or they could be bludgeoned into boredom. Which way it will go has little to do with students' actual ability; rather it results from a mix of teacher expectation and expertise, family background, and a great deal of luck.

The truth is, a reckless attitude that only some children can learn to high standards pervades education. Children who are slow to catch on to school at the beginning are not held to the same academic expectations as children whose home experiences give them a leg up at the outset. If all children were held to the same standards, schools would not tolerate nonreaders in the early grades, they would not bury most children in worksheets while "advanced" students tackled open-ended problems, they would not have persistent achievement gaps between groups of students. Yet this is the situation we typically find in U.S. schools.

We believe that all children can learn. And we believe that all children can learn well enough that by the end of sixth grade they will, among other things, be ready for algebra and be reading a daily newspaper with proficiency. Fortunately, what we believe is being proved in a small but growing number of schools where every child is expected to succeed and does—regardless of his or her family background or prior experiences. The challenge now is to repeat these successes in every elementary school across the country.

The Myth
of Unreadiness

A myth is by definition a story told to explain phenomena. The story in this case is that schools cannot teach children who come to school hungry, without parental care, undisciplined—even drug-addicted from birth.[1] Please note that the myth concerns the schools' response to these conditions. There is no dispute about how bad the conditions are for many children.

By the early 1990s, what we used to call "minority" children comprised the majority of elementary schoolchildren in four states— California, Texas, New Mexico, and Mississippi—and in most large urban districts.[2] This ratio is growing across the country. While some of these children embody the changing face of the American middle class, many others reflect the disproportionate impact that poverty has on African Americans, Native Americans, Latinos, and immigrants.[3]

At the end of the decade, 23 percent of the kindergarten class in U.S. schools came from single-parent families, 18 percent lived in families receiving welfare or food stamps, 14 percent had mothers who did not complete high school, and 9 percent spoke a language other than English as their primary language.[4] Researchers have related these "risk factors" to low academic achievement. They have further shown that the effect of such factors is cumulative: the more factors present, the greater the negative effect on performance. Beginning kindergartners with one risk factor are twice as likely as children with none to score at the bottom on tests of general knowledge and reading. Two or more risk factors triple their chance of ending up last. Indeed, the presence of risk factors seems to have a stronger relationship to low performance than their absence has to scoring at the top.[5]

These risk factors are relational, not causal. As we saw in eastern Pennsylvania, children who come to school under these conditions manage to achieve at the highest levels. But in most districts, the odds are still against them, brought on by schools that have only the lowest expectations that poor and minority children will achieve.

On the first day of school, two-thirds of our kindergartners can recognize their letters; nearly as many can count twenty objects.[6] What about the third who cannot? According to researchers Nicholas Zill and Jerry West:

> The [above] skills are not usually required for admission to kindergarten. Indeed, most kindergarten teachers feel that knowing letters and numbers is not crucial for school readiness because they can and do teach children these skills in kindergarten.... [But] developmental research indicates that children who have mastered these skills in the preschool years are more likely to learn to read, write and calculate earlier and more proficiently than those who have not.[7]

In the world of educators, all students can learn their letters and numbers. They can learn to write a paragraph and they can learn to calculate. But that's as far as many schools are willing to take them. The children who begin kindergarten behind tend to stay behind throughout their school careers. Nearly three out of every four African-American and Latino children come to school with one or more risk factors.[8] By fourth grade, only about one in ten children of color or from low-income families has learned to read well enough to routinely make inferences, draw conclusions, and make connections to their own experiences. Four times the number of their white peers have reached this level as have the children from middle- to high-income families.[9] The years in school actually increase this gap. To the country's shame, African-American and Latino high school seniors have only been taught to read and compute to the level of the average white thirteen-year-old.[10] The preconceived notions that these students' teachers had about their early abilities had become self-fulfilling. Their teachers taught them less. Small wonder that they learned little.

How All Is All?

In examining the desirability of national standards, the National Council on Education Standards and Testing (NCEST, discussed in chapter two) also had to consider how high and for whom. While the consensus for academic rigor was strong, the council was left with the sticky question of how to implement high standards when so many students at the time were struggling to meet low ones.

Considerable time and discussion were devoted to determining the feasibility of high standards for all students. Testimony was heard first about the special education populations, then about the students forced to attend poorly funded schools, followed by the children of non-English-speaking families and those in dysfunctional families and chaotic neighborhoods. Again and again, advocates posed the question, "Is it fair to hold these poor students to the same high standards as students with every home advantage?"

It was, as they say, a tough question. But two strong points of consensus finally emerged. First, it isn't fair to allow students to leave school without giving them the preparation they need to succeed in the world. By exempting children from high-level work on the basis of family circumstances, inadequate resources, or perceived "ability," schools are cruelly perpetuating the inequities children have already suffered. Second, when exceptions to "all students" are allowed, schools will find more and more children to exempt. This was how U.S. education got into this situation to begin with. Our schools produced a small number of high achievers and asked for only mediocre if not minimal results from the masses.

The council resolved to stop the flow of children into low-level courses and curriculum. In recommending national standards for all students, their intent was "to raise the ceiling for students who are currently above average and to lift the floor for those who now experience the least success in school, including those with special needs."[11] They included this powerful statement: "Poor initial performance should not be used to divert students into less demanding courses with lower expectations, but rather must lead to improved instruction and redoubled effort."[12]

The valuable work of NCEST disappeared in the intervening brouhaha over outcomes-based education and the conservative backlash against standards that we discussed earlier. It's a regrettable loss that delayed implementing their suggested reforms and denied another generation of students access to high-level knowledge and skills. But it's important to remind ourselves that, as we began the last decade, leaders from education, government, and business representing every constituency and ideology came to this consensus about national standards: High standards for all students. All students means all students. No more exceptions.

All Means All:

A Success Story

In 1999, Pine Spring Elementary School had one of the worst student performance records in the Virginia county where it's located. Virginia is one of the increasing number of states to institute a system of high standards for all students, aligned assessments, and school accountability for results. Pine Spring produced consistently low scores on the state assessment, the Standards of Learning (SOLs) and was in danger of falling short of the passing rate required for state accreditation. According to an article in the *Washington Post,* the district responded with an ultimatum: We will give you special funds to turn your performance around; if you fail, there will be consequences, which could mean replacing the whole staff.[13]

Although Pine Spring is located in an affluent suburban district, its students, drawn from a neighborhood of new immigrants, don't share the county's riches. Half of its students qualify for subsidized lunches and almost three-quarters come from homes where English isn't spoken. For too many years, these demographics were used to justify bad academic results. Then the state entered the picture demanding that schools prepare all of their students at least to the SOLs, or lose accreditation. The threat from the district superintendent only added more urgency to the task.

The district gave Pine Spring three years to improve. It took only one. The spring 2000 scores were three times over the district goal. Gains were reported in all grade levels and in all subjects on the state-designed SOLs and on the nationally normed Stanford 9. Fifth-graders went from a mediocre 64 percent passing the SOL math test in 1999 to 96 percent in 2000. In history they went from 29 percent to 89 percent passing.

The principal claimed no magic formula for their success. Instead, Pine Spring teachers told the *Post* reporter that "it was a lot of people pulling together." Administrators and faculty began by analyzing test scores to identify areas of strength and weakness at all levels—school, classroom, down to the individual child. One thing they discovered was that students seemed to understand math concepts, but their limited English was giving them difficulty with the word problems. The solution: teachers spent a lot of time on developing vocabulary. Teachers also planned together to make lessons more interesting for children and find ways to reinforce content by making connections across subjects. As their part, the school administrators found ways to improve the teacher-student ratio and hired more reading specialists.

Sometimes it takes a jolt of lightning to get people to see different possibilities. For Pine Spring Elementary, it took the threat of takeover. One teacher's comment about the turnaround was a clincher: "I had students telling me they'd never learned as much as they did last year." Children have a way of living up to the expectations adults have for them. We need to make sure we keep those expectations high.

2. ALL CHILDREN KNOW SOMETHING

Schools continue to treat children's minds as empty vessels waiting to be filled by teachers. An example is reading. In the early grades children are usually taught letters and sounds—B is for *buhh*, C is for *ssss* and *kuhh*, and so on—and shown how to identify beginning, then ending, and finally middle sounds in simple words, such as *dog* and *cat*. They are read to by their teachers out of big books and follow the teacher's finger as she or he points to the words. Later they will on their own begin to read simple books leveled to their growing reading vocabulary. But in most early elementary classrooms the emphasis is still on the isolated development of so-called decoding skills—an emphasis most parents can testify to by the volume of worksheets their children bring home.

On the surface, there doesn't appear to be much wrong with this picture. Most children benefit from explicit phonics instruction as well as opportunities to read and be read to. But remember our story about Andrew in chapter one. Most of Andrew's classmates knew their letters before entering kindergarten. Assuming they are like the majority of five-year-olds, they also knew that letters make words, words appear in books, and books make stories. And they probably knew that books are organized from left to right.

In short, Andrew's classmates arrived at school knowing a lot about reading, even if they did not yet know *how* to read. The emphasis on skill development independent from reading real books works for these children because they already understand that putting sounds to symbols will unlock the key to the grown-up world of books. On their own, they are supplying meaning and purpose to the task.

Andrew on the other hand had almost no experience with the printed word. He did not know his letters and was not aware that books held stories. When his teachers gave him phonics worksheets, he was clueless about their purpose. The teachers' response to his confusion was more worksheets and simple books written to formula. The more interesting work would have to come later.

Andrew's teachers thought that he had only deficits in his knowledge bank. What they failed to recognize was that while Andrew didn't understand printed text, he knew a lot about stories. He knew the conventions of a beginning, middle, and end. He could make predictions and draw inferences about characters. As he grew older, he learned about mathematics from sports and about problem solving through computer games. But these random, unschool-like attributes were not valued in the classroom.

Unfortunately for Andrew, no one saw the opportunity to connect what he knew on his own to what he needed to learn to become fully literate. Instead it was assumed he didn't have the background to move forward academically when in fact he knew a lot. What he lacked was structure and context to help him understand the baffling work of school.

One out of three beginning kindergartners doesn't know their letters. Close to one in five doesn't know the conventions of print or the point where a story ends in a book.[14] Within this group are a sizable number of children who are unable to process letter-sound combinations. These children may be in the minority, but they still represent large numbers. Schools across the country have shown that students such as these can be successfully taught and become proficient readers and budding mathematicians and scientists. But in most classrooms such children are consigned to the dump heap of low expectations.

After years of frustration in the classroom, children like Andrew feel stupid and bored. By fourth grade many of them have already begun to drop out even though they still physically occupy space. The quiet ones daydream, the more assertive kids become discipline problems. They could have been directed toward engaging schoolwork and high-level content, if only someone had understood how smart these children really are.

The Fallacy of Skills
First, Meaning After

The emphasis on the development of skills before engaging in rich and interesting content had a devastating effect on Andrew's schooling. But in this regard he wasn't alone. Most of his classmates knew a lot about reading and were developing a fairly good sense of numbers before they entered kindergarten. So what did their teachers do? Gave them coloring activities and number and letter games that cover information they already understood or were able to learn quickly.

American education operates under the assumption that mastery of basic skills must precede content. As a result, we are doing a fairly good job at teaching basic skills. By the time our youngsters are in high school, virtually all of them have learned to decode written language and perform whole number computations with accuracy. But our students are not making the leap to higher levels of performance. Very few high school seniors have learned to comprehend complex texts or solve open-ended problems calling for multiple steps.[15] The breakdown already shows by fourth grade. Only one in four nine-year-olds is able to determine the appropriate mathematical operation to use when analyzing a word problem—a task that requires both mathematical problem solving and proficient reading comprehension.[16]

Much has been said over the last ten years about the importance of critical thinking, problem solving, and other "higher order thinking skills," which, typical of education vernacular, comes with the terminally cute acronym HOTS. We have already mentioned thinking skills in our listing of the standards, where we point out that if the subject matter is taught adequately, HOTS will be developed without special training.

The leading proponents of thinking skills came from business, industry, and universities who were complaining about the weak abilities of high school graduates. In response, the education research community came back with programs in "thinking" that were added on to the skills-first, content-later (or never) curriculum. It was a solution much like trying to plaster over the cracks in a wall rotten inside with dampness.

The domain of cognitive research, on the other hand, has established that what is called higher order thinking in actuality governs learning from the first. As Lauren Resnick writes,

> The most important single message of modern research on the nature of thinking is that the kinds of activities traditionally associated with thinking are not limited to advanced levels of development.... [R]esearch suggests that failure to cultivate aspects of thinking such as

those listed in our working definition of higher order skills may be the source of major learning difficulties even in elementary school.[17]

Resnick's list (widely cited and now all but universally accepted) describes thinking as nonalgorithmic, complex, yielding multiple solutions, involving nuanced judgment, applying multiple criteria, uncertain, self-regulating, imposing meaning, and effortful.

Children have been thinking since their first moment of consciousness, and from the age of toddling they have been learning to construct language with increasing sophistication. By the time they enter school they are usually speaking in reasonably well-conceived sentences—and can tell a pretty good tale besides.

Nevertheless, in the perverse manner of schools, spelling and syntax are taught as the precursors to writing, not as its refinement. Open-ended math problems are assigned as "extra credit" after the drills and worksheets are done. And analytical discussions are too often relegated to the book club or held in reserve for the "gifted and talented" students. The very practices that would help struggling students most by giving them a context for learning skills are withheld for the students who already understand the connections.

The misguided practice of focusing lessons on the discrete development of skills without content makes it difficult for children to connect their work to real learning. In addition, it wastes valuable classroom time that would be more efficiently spent advancing the whole class with mutually reinforcing lessons linking skill to content, and vice versa. Teachers must recognize that children enter the classroom with an abundance of raw material that should be enlarged with more content and given form with skills.

Authentic Instruction—
Learning in Context

Following the same line of research as Lauren Resnick, Fred Newmann, Gary Wehlage, and their associates at the University of Wisconsin–Madison not only recognize that all children know something and bring it to school with them, but also that authentic intellectual work includes connecting school with life outside[18]. Newmann and Wehlage point out that school-work often seems "contrived and artificial," a judgment we shall reinforce in the next section of this chapter. On the other hand, the work of skilled adults (not servers in McDonald's using symbols instead of numbers to add up charges) seems meaningful and significant. The two define the work students should be doing in school in these words:

> Authentic intellectual work, involves original application of knowledge and skills (rather than just routine use of facts and procedures). … We summarize these distinctive characteristics of authentic intellectual work as three criteria: construction of knowledge; through the use of disciplined inquiry; to produce discourse, products, or performances that have value beyond school.[19]

Authentic intellectual work in English/language arts can be illustrated using one of the most common assignments even in early grades, the book report. Students are usually rewarded for simple plot summaries. Instead, they should be asked to respond to "why" questions: Why do you like (or dislike) this book? Why did the main character take a specific action? Why does the author tell you certain details? Further, they should compare the book to others they have read. And, to bring the assignment back to their lives, they should be asked to compare it to the reality they know: Could this have happened? Have you every experienced a similar event?

Such an approach would have built on Andrew's love and knowledge of stories and helped him to develop logical abilities and increased his desire to read.

In mathematics, students should be asked to use their skills to understand their environment. Instead of a worksheet on measurement, they should be asked—depending on the grade level—to use various units of measurement, including their own bodies: how many feet, literally, does it take to measure the distance between the door and the wall of the classroom? How many of Juanita's feet and how many of Mr. Palmer's feet? What does this mean in terms of needing a standard measurement? Is it smart to try to measure the school corridor with a ruler, or should we use a yardstick? Why? What about the distance between school and home (or a local landmark such as a shopping center or amusement park)?

Children in fourth grade who are presented with worksheets asking them to do multiplications of numbers ending in zeros (yes, we've seen them) are ten years old. They have already been negotiating prices, paying fares on public transportation, responding to advertising, *using* mathematics every day outside the classroom for years. This experience must be honored and built on as a foundation for inquiry, not buried by an avalanche of disconnected worksheets. Elementary students should be full of questions, and their teachers should encourage them to seek the answers from the whole of their experience, in and out of school.

Wasting Children's Time

The belief that children come to school knowing nothing is conspicuously seen in what passes for social studies in the early grades. Known as "expanding horizons," or sometimes "expanding environments," this curriculum is based on a belief that children need to learn about the world beginning with what is most immediate and present—themselves—and "expand" their outlook from there. Over the first three grades, the horizons expand from family to school, neighborhood, and finally community. They are topics most children are already expert on by the time they enter kindergarten.

Education historian and critic Diane Ravitch could find no basis in research for the expanding horizons curriculum. Her survey of leading scholars in cognitive psychology, child development, and curriculum theory revealed that "[n]one knew of any research justifying the expanding environments approach; none defended it. All deplored the absence of historical and cultural content in the early grades."[20]

Despite this information, it remains the prevailing curriculum in elementary school. And teachers' hold on this approach is formidable. The committee writing the national history standards was made to compromise with the early childhood educators by forcing U.S. and world history into an expanding horizons framework of family, neighborhood, and community. In Virginia the first draft of social studies standards was roundly condemned by early elementary teachers for expecting young students to learn real history. To this day, many Virginia teachers insist that their third-graders aren't ready or able to learn about ancient Egypt and China.[21]

The persistent view that children know nothing—even about family and neighborhood—unless schools teach it to them is a gross underestimation of children's capacities. Remarkably, for educators concerned with youngsters, it completely disarms children of their power of imagination.

In *Teaching as Story Telling,* Kieran Egan criticizes the near absence of history in the expanding horizons curriculum. Referring to what he calls an ad hoc principle of moving outward from "present, local experience to the unknown," Egan asks: "If this [principle] is true, how can we explain children's easy engagement with star warriors, wicked-witches, and talking middle-class worms?"[22]

But just as grappling with real literature is withheld from students until they demonstrate their ability with decoding, so is history reserved for the upper elementary grades, by which time many children have been anesthetized into indifference. The pity is that history, replete with heroes, adventure, and faraway places, can captivate the imaginations of young children as easily as fairy tales and legends do.

Schools waste children's time. History is taught as a content-less look at what students already know. Reading is as much, or more, a fill-in-the-box, connect-the-dots-and-lines exercise as it is an encounter with books. Writing is lists of spelling words, grammar worksheets, journal entries with no purpose, an occasional personal response, and lots of coloring. Science, if it exists at all, is a hit-and-run with lessons teachers like—one month it's butterflies, in spring we do dinosaurs, the fifth grade gets to play with pond water—that bear little connection to each other or to learning real science concepts.

In a TV commercial widely screened in summer 2000, a young woman who is a teacher is buying school supplies for her (we hope) elementary classroom.[23] Her husband complains about the effect on their household budget but relents as both buy crayons and glue and scissors in an office supply store. The teacher says plaintively, "The children need those supplies."

We long to shout at the screen, "No they don't!" At least not as many. Making things takes up far too much time in elementary school. We have seen teachers ostensibly teaching writing who teach children carefully to fold paper, punch it, thread colored wool through to make a spine, and then decorate the cover not only with drawings but also with stick-on stars and spangles (those school supplies). Then the children laboriously copy a few sentences into the "book." In the time taken up by the bookmaking, they could write twice as much.

One of the most egregious examples we have seen was a mathematics assignment for third-graders. They were told the principle of motion-picture cartoons—that the illusion of movement is created by a series of drawings that differ slightly from one another and are then moved so fast that the images seem to be moving. The children made a series of pictures, each slightly different from the other, punched a hole in each, and strung them onto a metal ring (more school supplies). This activity, taking days of mathematics time, was intended to help them understand the answer to this problem: If six pictures are needed for each second, how many pictures do you need for half a minute of moving cartoon?

It is obviously useful and important for children to know how moving cartoons are made, but a demonstration by the teacher would have been enough. And third-graders should know their multiplication tables, as we saw in the mathematics standards, so that the mathematical challenge is lacking here.

One suspects that this idea came either from a textbook, or from a "make and take" workshop at a teachers conference, where teachers learn "cute" tricks using old milk and egg cartons. Students do not need to make a caterpillar out of an egg carton with pipe-cleaner antennae—all painted green—to write about the metamorphosis of butterflies.

Elementary school keeps children busy. But the work is boring. Just ask the next ten-year-old you see.

3. TEACHERS ARE CENTRAL TO STUDENTS' LEARNING

For several years researchers have been examining the relationship between various factors and student achievement. We have already discussed many of these. Students who come from poor families or who are minorities tend to perform at low levels. We also saw how young children who come from single-parent families, whose primary language is not English, or whose mothers did not complete high school enter kindergarten already burdened with so-called risk factors.

Because these factors concern children's lives outside of school, many educators and researchers have concluded that schools can do little to make a difference in their academic performance. This view was first made in 1966 by sociologist James S. Coleman, who claimed that family background explained most of the disparity in achievement between white and minority students in U.S. schools.

Repercussions from Coleman and his disciples continue to be felt today. Having been told again and again that family, race, and economic status matter most, educators have been led to believe that the educational progress of many of their students is out of their control.

Nothing could be further from the truth. Teachers matter a lot.

More recent research has shown that of all the variables relating to student achievement, teachers account for the single greatest share: more than family background, mother's education level, or primary language. Harvard researcher Ronald Ferguson estimates that schools control at least 50 percent of all factors related to student achievement.[24] According to economist Eric Hanushek, "The difference between a good and a bad teacher can be a full grade level of achievement in a single school year."[25]

Some researchers find even greater differences. Important studies out of Tennessee and Dallas, Texas, have related teacher effectiveness to student achievement. *Effective* in these analyses is defined quite simply: teachers whose students make the most gains on a standardized assessment. The researchers tracked the progress of cohorts of elementary students who scored at about the same level on the state tests. Three years later, they found that children who had three consecutive "effective" teachers significantly outscored their peers who had the misfortune to be assigned to three "ineffective" teachers in a row. The difference? A whopping 50 percentile points.

Kati Haycock, the director of the Education Trust, writes, "Differences of this magnitude ... are stunning. As all of us know only too well, they can represent the difference between a remedial label and placement in the accelerated or even gifted track. And the difference between entry into a selective college and a lifetime at McDonald's."[26]

The effective-teacher research adds fuel to the already active standards movement. More evidence of the importance of teachers has emerged in studies of high-performing, high-poverty schools that attribute their success to high expectations and no excuses for student failure.[27] By showing that schools make a difference even with so-called at-risk students, many policy makers and advocates are better able to counter the naysayers and insist that high standards are for all students. As we mentioned in chapter two, almost every state has in place or is working on a system of high standards, aligned assessments, and accountability for results. States that have led the nation in implementing standards are showing dramatic gains. In Texas and North Carolina, for example, all students are making tremendous progress at the same time gaps between groups of students are narrowing, particularly those between students in low-income and affluent districts.[28]

The major resource for students' success is teachers' professional skill. But we are now asking teachers to do something they weren't necessarily prepared to do: teach all students to levels that only a few have reached up until now. For this reason, the preparation and professional development of teachers are our most pressing needs.

Who's Teaching the Children?

Our current teaching force can't be expected to change their teaching techniques without enlarging their repertoire, trying out new ideas, refining them, and being allowed time for all this. No one is doing a poor job on purpose.

Most of the teachers in U.S. elementary schools do not have degrees in an academic subject.[29] They have degrees in education, so methods courses displaced academic subjects from their program. Furthermore, many of these methods courses, especially those taken by veteran teachers, were based on an outmoded understanding of human cognition.[30] Teachers were educated to think of knowledge as a ladder students climb with skills. As we have shown, it's widely held in schools that skills must precede knowledge. From this view of cognition as a ladder—with only a vague sense of where the ladder reaches—naturally flow basal readers, tracking, worksheets, and the detachment from the real world that children sense immediately in school.

Instead, cognitive science has established that "human minds are constructed to deal with richly complex environments, to make sense out of their experiences, and to store knowledge that is useful in coping with new ones."[31] Even our youngest students are analyzing and synthesizing new information. The standards summarized in chapter three reflect these abilities by calling on students to, for example, reason, interpret, discuss, and explain the subject matter.

But the message that cognition is an active search to understand the world hasn't reached elementary education. Teachers for the most part still operate on the principle that skills must be learned and tested before children can approach knowledge. Making change even more difficult, parents expect this kind of skill-ladder teaching because they were taught that way themselves and can see no reason why their children shouldn't go through the same process.

Overall, content knowledge is undervalued in the preparation of elementary teachers. Not only do academic courses take a backseat to methodology, the examinations elementary teachers take to become licensed are concerned mostly with pedagogy. The only test of academic content that prospective elementary teachers take is a basic literacy examination that most states require for all teachers, secondary included. Of these, the most widely used tests have been found to address subject matter that never exceeds the tenth-grade level. Many of the items test middle-school content, especially in mathematics.[32] Despite the low level of these examinations, thousands of prospective teachers fail them every year.

The short shrift given subject matter in the preparation of elementary teachers can have severe and long-lasting repercussions. Researchers have identified a strong relationship between teachers' verbal and mathematics skills and their students' academic performance. Teachers who score high on either basic literacy tests or their college admissions tests tend to produce students who also score high on state assessments.[33]

Using the vast Texas database, Ferguson was able to identify and compare districts with low-scoring teachers and above-average early elementary students to districts with the opposite situation, high-scoring teachers and below-average elementary students. By eleventh grade, the pattern of achievement flip-flopped. The students who began elementary school below average but with high-scoring teachers were now above average. The reverse was also true: students who began school above average but with low-scoring teachers had fallen to below-average status by high school.[34] Read this paragraph again if you need to. The findings are staggering.

A Different Kind of Classroom

The following passage describes what school is like for some second-grade bilingual children in a school in the heart of the Navajo Nation in Arizona:

> Two children were huddled at the computer keyboard composing a report about Japanese exports. They were discussing at which point

it would be most effective to insert a chart of data base information. The teacher assistant was listening to a group of six children who planned to present a choral reading of Shel Silverstein's "Ladies First" to the first grade. Jamie was listening to Terri read *Chocolate Fever*—"Just skip that word. It'll make sense later," he said when she hesitated. Several children sat with their writing folders and revised pieces or used editing checklists. Mara proudly added "use quotation marks" to the Things I Do Well list at the back of her writing folder. Johnson was adding the word "displacement" to his personal dictionary.... Two more children were busy measuring sticks for a building project: they recorded notations of the length and width of the sticks. Johnny was standing on a table with binoculars looking out the window.[35]

A drawing of this scene would not be immediately recognizable as a picture of a school. It shares features (perhaps with the exception of the child standing on the table) with a busy office where people are engaged in cooperative tasks. And that is precisely the point: the stereotype of the school has been broken.

In the past the instruction remained constant. All students in the class were fed the same activities at the same time. At assessment time, student achievement varied. And the class as a whole moved on to the next unit.

In a standards-based system, the standard, or expected student achievement, is the constant. Instruction therefore must vary. Assessment in this model is ongoing and diagnostic. Students who meet the standard move on. Students who don't meet the standard are retaught until they do, if necessary with new approaches. Thus the Navajo classroom is seen to be a place where all students are doing different things, but all are working toward standards.

We can't underestimate what the simple act of demanding high standards for all students can do. When everyone knows that first-graders are expected to be writing reports and fourth-graders are expected to be competent with simple fractions and percents, for example, all of a sudden students who were never before given the chance are writing reports and doing fractions. As a result, in places where standards have been implemented, low-achieving students benefit first and show the most gains.

At the same time we must acknowledge that the simple act is, in reality, not simple. Education school for most practicing teachers did not prepare them to manage a standards-based classroom. True, Andrew's teachers should have expected more for him. But in their defense, they probably were not taught strategies for accelerating learning in children like Andrew.

The shift to standards is not going to be complete without a massive investment in professional development. In addition, schools need a whole different view of what professional development looks like. Present professional development programs are typically hit-or-miss affairs devoting maybe one, maybe three hours to learning new techniques such as co-operative learning or learning styles. The treatment is at best superficial. There is no follow-up as teachers try to implement new strategies in the classroom. What little effect professional development has tends to be cosmetic. It may look new, but the core is the same old practice with the same old results.

Effective professional development is ongoing and driven by the standards students are expected to meet. The school needs to support teachers by structuring time in the regular schedule for meetings with colleagues, by providing technical assistance when needed, and by encouraging a spirit of shared purpose. Teachers are central to learning. In order to be successful, professional development must be made central to teaching.

LOOKING AT
TEACHERS' WORK

A common and often highly regarded form of professional development is called looking at student work. While student work should be the object of scrutiny, the looking should be done in the context of the assignment and the standards. We prefer to look at teachers' work first to see what the students were asked to do.[36] Our approach is based on an important truth: *Students can do no better than the assignments they are given.*

Recent research in California confirms the importance of assignments. DataWorks Educational Research was examining the reasons for poor performance in schools in California's Intermediate Intervention/Under-Performing Schools Program. After looking at all the data they could collect for two years, the researchers finally asked for all the work students did in one week in the schools they were examining.

Although they were looking at the student work, in fact they were inferring teachers' assignments from the work. They aligned the pieces with the California standards (downloaded, as almost all state standards can be, from the Internet). They marked each piece of work with the appropriate grade-level standard—"GLS 3," for example.

Their analysis showed that only kindergarten and first-grade students were getting assignments aligned with their GLS. At second grade the slippage below the standards began. By fifth grade the slippage was so bad that only 2 percent of the assignments were on grade level. Most of what the students were being asked to do was appropriate for second or third grade. When the researchers reported their findings to one school, "in a single moment, the 48 employees, in unison, understood what 'teaching to the standards' meant."[37] Or as one principal said to us in another state, "We've been teaching the wrong things."

Silvia Ybarra and John Hollingsworth, the DataWorks researchers, didn't stop with reporting their findings. They recommended that the school adopt a new mission statement: "All instruction at this school will be at grade-level according to the California standards." The teachers should stamp every assignment with the appropriate GLS, and the school should redirect all professional development toward teaching at grade level.

One of their recommendations is especially reminiscent of those offered by Resnick and Newmann and Wehlage (amazing how researchers converge on the same recommendations!). They suggest that teachers forget "remediating" students or going slowly so that they will catch up if necessary, but instead they should teach all students at the standards level:

> In the fourth grade, for example, teach multiple-paragraph compositions right from the start as opposed to teaching them where they are (i.e., repeating single sentences or single paragraphs).
>
> If by the end of third grade, for example, students still have not learned the multiplication tables after good instruction, extended learning time, and support, change the instructional practices. If students still have problems, provide them with a times table "cheat sheet" so that they can move on and not be stuck repeating the 3rd grade-level standards forever and ever.[38]

If professional development sessions consisted only of aligning teachers' assignments and student work, they would be invaluable in terms of student challenge and excitement—not to mention achievement—in the classroom.

4. INSTRUCTION
SHOULD BE BALANCED

Our fourth principle is the most altered from the original set we defined nine years ago. At the time we wrote the first edition of *Smart Start* in 1991, educators, policy makers, and pundits were engaged in a holy war over "multicultural education." On the one side were advocates for ethnocentric curriculums—subject matter, especially the humanities, taught from the point of view of groups outside the mainstream—that were promoted as a means to boost the self-image of minority students and make their schooling meaningful. On the other side were traditionalists who perceived multiculturalism as a threat to the sanctity of the canon and the preservation of Western values. Each side, it seemed, was intent on demonizing the other.

In an attempt to calm tempers and return the focus to Americans' shared goals, we established our fourth guiding principle: *E pluribus unum*—"out of many, one." We argued that children should have a curriculum that encompasses both diversity and the common culture. Every group, country, and era has produced good literature. The works we feature in chapter three include both Western and non-Western children's literature. In addition, understanding different perspectives is a fundamental skill for historical thinking. Students should be encouraged to look at events through the eyes of different groups as well as their own. This ability, we asserted, strengthens rather than thwarts democratic values.

We called for balance.

By the end of the decade, the battle over multicultural education had lost some of its passion. U.S. schoolchildren learn about Timbuktu alongside ancient Greece, and the Republic still stands. But to our surprise the holy war continues. Almost any issue, it seems, becomes the occasion for another battle between traditionalists and progressives.

The education community contributes to the hostilities. Education is infected with a kind of dichotomous thinking, especially when it involves methods of instruction. When confronted with a new piece of research, schools all too frequently react by believing that if the new thing is good, the old thing must therefore be bad, regardless of whether some of it was working well, and often before the new ideas are sufficiently tested.

This tendency gives factions plenty of reason to draw battle lines. Incredibly, issues about instructional methods have worked their way into political campaigns, and local school-board meetings have become arenas for sheer viciousness in public debate. Drop in sometime when they're adopting a new reading series!

We now see that the balance we advised for multicultural education is sorely missing from much of what happens in our schools. This has led us to enlarge our original fourth principle to: Instruction should be balanced. Below we discuss some of the hot-button issues that would greatly benefit from a balanced view. Some of these have caught fire in the public domain. Others are held closer within the education community. In every case, each side has merit, but neither side has the complete answer.

The Reading Wars

Parents and pundits have been railing about the absence of phonics instruction since Rudolph Flesch published his indictment of look-say instruction, *Why Johnny Can't Read*, in 1955. But it took the "whole language" movement to elevate reading instruction to a full-blown political issue by pitting itself against the "phonics first and furious" crowd.

Earlier we declined to take sides in this war because the standards have made a sensible compromise and the excellent guides to reading instruction we cited there have sensible ways to a workable truce. To recap briefly, phonics refers to the development of putting sounds to letters and syllables taught through explicit discrete instruction. Whole language takes a holistic approach through writing and through reading whole texts, deemphasizing direct skill instruction.

Everyone acknowledges the importance of reading to future academic success, which is probably why the reading wars have been among the ugliest. They have also marked the clearest lines between the pro-family conservatives on one side and the educational establishment on the other. The level of paranoia has been so high that members of each faction have at some point charged the others of a conspiracy to hold down the lower classes by deliberately keeping them illiterate and thereby retaining their own economic advantage (to paraphrase Dave Barry, we are not making this up).

While the attacks and counterattacks from extremists on both sides provided some mild entertainment, the battle itself was no laughing matter. As with most wars, the innocents were caught in the crossfire; in this case, the emerging readers who were being jerked back and forth whenever a new camp gained control.

Then in the mid-1990s, research from the National Institute of Child Development and Health (NICDH) emerged that has helped to quell the debate, at least somewhat. This unlikely source sponsored several studies and literature reviews on reading and reading failure. The credibility of NICDH on the topic is perhaps not so unlikely—an outside authority was needed, one not involved in educational politics.

Their findings stressed the importance of explicit instruction in phonics and phonological awareness *and* a "major emphasis on reading and writing in environments that include good literature, reading for enjoyment, and other practices believed to facilitate the development of reading skills and literacy."[39] They further found that "the NICDH studies are consistent with educational research highlighting the importance of *balanced* [their emphasis] approaches to reading instruction."[40]

Children need to learn to decode text, certainly. They also need to build vocabulary, to comprehend what they read, to read critically and analytically. These abilities need to be developed simultaneously. So whole language or phonics? Both, of course.[41]

The Math Wars

A cynic might be tempted to think that because multiculturalism failed to end democracy as we know it, and NICDH pronounced the final word on reading, the traditionalists had no place to go but to attack mathematics. But we are not cynics, so we accept their criticism of the National Council of Teachers of Mathematics (NCTM) standards as genuine concern over the direction of mathematics instruction. But first we must back up again to the beginning of the last decade and revisit the NCEST hearings one more time.

When national leaders began to debate the desirability and feasibility of national standards, mathematics was the only subject to have undergone a consensus-building process of defining what students should know and be able to do at fourth, eighth, and twelfth grades.[42] These standards were drafted because of the initiative and foresight of the NCTM, which thought it was time to reevaluate what was most important in their discipline. NCEST members and reform leaders praised the NCTM standards for being models, first for elevating the mathematical expectations for all students, and second for responding to a changing world and the mathematics it will require for work and citizenship. The math standards subsequently had a profound influence on textbooks, state standards documents, and the content of standardized assessments, including National Assessment of Educational Progress.

It was not mathematics as usual. The NCTM standards emphasized problem solving, the ability to communicate mathematically, and a conceptual understanding of numbers and number theory. All students would need to know algebra, geometry, and statistics and probability. They would be expected to move easily among different operations and domains according to the needs of the situation. They would be able to manipulate data with confidence. Words such as *estimate* and *use calculators* were prominent. Unfortunately, words such as *addition facts* and *multiplication tables* were not. Rather, the drafters assumed that anyone using the standards for computation would automatically understand that they require knowing how to add, subtract, multiply, and divide with accuracy. They assumed wrong.

By mid-decade, members of the Mathematical Association of America were grumbling about the deemphasis of algorithms in the NCTM standards. A California group claiming to represent mathematicians and parents, called Mathematically Correct, began issuing position statements condemning "fuzzy math" and the "new new math." The opposition took out full-page ads in the *Washington Post* and *Education Week* blasting integrated math programs.

NCTM proponents weren't helped by members within their own ranks who insisted that "real mathematical power, on the one hand, and facility with multidigit, pencil-and-paper computational algorithms, on the other, are mutually exclusive.... [C]ontinuing to teach these skills ... is counterproductive and downright dangerous."[43]

Two points: By deemphasizing memorization and drill in the standards, many educators responded by throwing out everything they had always done even though they had not yet sufficiently developed their own skill with teaching math in a new way. Despite this, the new standards are beginning to have a positive effect. After being flat for some time, math achievement, though still not where it should be, is improving.[44]

Second, it's important to note that the criticism is coming mostly from research mathematicians, the pure mathematicians in universities. Those who use applied mathematics—industry leaders, engineers, scientists, and social scientists—have not entered the fight for the most part. Could it be that in stressing the practical applications of mathematics the NCTM standards promise to better prepare students for the math they need in the real world? We think the input of these professionals would make a significant contribution to resolving the conflict.

As with reading, a good mathematics program is neither this nor that. It integrates skills and critical thinking, isolated drill and open-ended problems, the abstract and real-world applications. But the emphasis must always be on building a deep conceptual understanding.

NCTM has revised and updated its 1989 standards. In the new version, accuracy and math facts are made explicit. They are no longer implied and left to chance. But the war still rages, and once again it's the students who suffer.

Multiple Intelligences

How is it that certain research catches on like wildfire? Educators seem particularly infatuated with brain research. For a while there was the left brain/right brain craze. Then early childhood teachers got into cognitive "hardwiring." We do not intend to diminish the enormous strides science is making in the study of the human mind. We do wish to observe, however, that when educators attempt to adapt brain theory to instruction, they usually end up proving the dictum that a little bit of knowledge is a dangerous thing.

The theory of multiple intelligences (MI) surely falls into this category. In the 1980s, Harvard psychologist Howard Gardner identified seven different "intelligences," significantly expanding on our traditional notion of intelligence as being largely verbal and computational.[45] In addition to what he calls the linguistic and logical-mathematical intelligences, Gardner further contends that intelligence manifests through musical ability, spatial or visual sense, physical movement (bodily-kinesthetic), and interpersonal and intrapersonal relations. Gardner has since added an eighth intelligence: naturalist, or the ability to interact with and understand the natural world.[46]

Gardner's theory validates what parents and teachers know instinctively: that children vary in their strengths and weaknesses. Within the same family you will typically find the artistic one, or the athlete, or the social butterfly. It's telling that we refer to the logical child as the "smart one." Gardner's theory, then, allows us to recognize and value these other strengths. He further maintains that we all possess each of the intelligences, but in different degrees. Strength in one area, therefore, should not preclude strength in another. Nor should it suggest that being weak in one intelligence means that intelligence cannot be developed.

The theory of multiple intelligences is provocative and could have some worthwhile implications for instruction and assessment. Gardner's present work, in fact, is focusing on precisely that. Unfortunately, in the meantime, the eight intelligences have swept through the professional development workshop circuit with hurricane force. Armed with the most superficial understanding, teachers now feel compelled to address the needs of these different kinds of learners. And the most idiotic acts are being committed in the name of multiple intelligences.

We found a recommended lesson plan on an MI web page that perfectly illustrates the pitfalls of this theory in practice. This fifth-grade science lesson was designed to help students learn about and compare main types of energy sources. Teachers were to set up eight separate "centers" corresponding to each of the eight intelligences. Students would select one activity at one center to complete. It wasn't clear whether students chose their "intelligence" center or the teacher made the assignment for them. It should be noted that this is fairly typical format for proposed MI lessons.

Altogether, there were eighteen activities spread across the centers. We list just a few to give a flavor of the range of challenge and content. "Naturalists" could write a compare-and-contrast paper on two energy sources, or play an energy source matching game with cards. The bodily, kinesthetic learner could pantomime an energy source; team members would get to guess which one. Visual learners could construct a pie chart of energy use statistics; the statistics were provided, actual research apparently being the province of the logical learner. Ah, but the logical learner could line up dominoes to model a nuclear chain reaction (instructions: "knock over the first domino and notice what happens"), or compute high tides for a week based on two days' data. The verbal learner could write a persuasive essay. The musical learner could compose a persuasive rap.[47]

Unfortunately, there are no scoring guides provided for these activities. We would be very interested to know how a teacher is supposed to evaluate whether plopping given numbers into a pie chart shows the same depth of understanding about energy sources as writing a compare-and-contrast paper.

Such inanity is not restricted to elementary school. A high school chemistry teacher in Virginia once told us how she gave her eleventh-grade students refrigerator magnet letters and numbers—the same kind preschool children play with—and instructed them to use the magnets to form the chemistry formulas in their textbook. She thought this would engage the "kinesthetic learners" in her overactive class. This was in December, at which point the students had still not been allowed in the chemistry lab. The teacher told us they needed to learn their formulas first. She would have been much more successful if she quit treating them like babies and taught them some real chemistry. But that might have privileged the "logical learners."

At every level of schooling, we see no end of coloring assignments, pantomimes, and diamante poems taking the place of substantial work. What's worse, some Gardner enthusiasts are coming perilously close to instituting an elaborate but equally damaging form of tracking. We once angered a self-described MI disciple during a presentation in which we stressed the importance of writing in different modes. "But that's not fair to the visual learner!" she cried. We asked what activities she would assign for those students. "Posters," she said.

On some planet, posters, expository jingles, and interpretive dance might help certain students understand complex concepts. But they are not the media that either colleges or the working world rely on for communication in their day-to-day business. Despite this, too many teachers believe that assignments such as these are helping the nonlinguistic, nonlogical learner, when in fact they are preventing many students from competing.

Gardner has recognized how his theory is being misused. He writes: "[M]any educators see MI theory as an end in itself.... But enhancing 'multiple intelligences' is not in itself a suitable goal of education. Rather, it is better thought of as a handmaiden to good education, once educational goals have been established on independent grounds."[48]

All students need to develop the knowledge and skills that will prepare them for success in college and careers. Standards define what these are. Acknowledging multiple intelligences in curriculum design can be helpful for students with various learning styles in addition to helping all students converse competently in a multimedia world. But, as the man said, MI is not the end itself.

Ability Grouping

In the first edition of *Smart Start*, we took a rather hard stance against ability grouping. There was a good reason for this. Ability grouping as it tends to be practiced in schools differs little from a rigid tracking system. Children who are placed in low-ability reading and math groups in first grade rarely get out, and low expectations follow them through middle and high school, as we saw in Andrew's case.

Standards allow us to reevaluate our hard-line position on ability grouping. Robert Slavin, a longtime critic of tracking and ability grouping, has put his research into practice with the highly effective Success for All program.[49] While he condemns the use of self-contained classes and other rigid demarcations based on ability, he recognizes the instructional value of using temporary, flexible grouping to work with students with similar needs. He recommends that successful ability groups would have these features:

- Students' primary assignment is in a heterogeneous class. Students are regrouped by ability only when it's important to learning.

- Grouping is based on specific skills and not general achievement level or IQ.

- Students are frequently assessed and regrouped accordingly.

- The pace and level of instruction varies according to the needs of the group (but not the standard).

- Only a small number of groups should be formed with a class.[50]

When standards are the same for all students, the burden is on the school to find ways to make sure students will meet them. Teachers and administrators must be free to use every trick they have to help a variety of learners. As long as all of its students are performing to high levels it doesn't really matter which approach the school takes to reading and mathematics, or whether teachers temporarily group students who are having difficulty with certain skills. What matters is that no child is allowed to fall through the cracks.

Special Needs Children: "Learning Disabled" and Mainstreaming

Ability groups within a classroom can allow teachers to attend to the needs of children who learn at different speeds. In chapter five, we shall see two examples of ability groupings that permit teaching to children's needs and are also very fluid, so that a child does not stay in a group that is moving slowly if he or she has picked up speed. Ability groups can be justified as ways to increase efficiency in teaching and learning. What continues to exercise our incredulity is the continued use of special classifications—the kind that result from psychological tests and can brand children for life.

While we acknowledged in 1991 that the special needs of some students require different handling, we were alarmed, and still are, over the numbers of children set up as exceptions. Over the last two decades, the number of students classified as disabled has increased from 8 percent of enrollments in 1977 to 13 percent in 1998. Most of the increase is attributable to labeling more children as learning disabled: from barely 2 percent of the student population to the current 6 percent.[51]

The classification as "learning disabled" and therefore needing special education is problematic. Learning disabilities seem to vary from severe dyslexia to emotional problems that prevent children from paying sufficient attention in class. The classification is fuzzy enough to suggest that some children are labeled because they are difficult to deal with in classrooms rather than objectively disabled. The percentage of children who cannot learn in the same classrooms because of severe disabilities—blindness and deafness, for example—is not more than 3 percent of the population.

In order to give as many students as possible the same education, school districts have adopted the policy of "mainstreaming" children who are labeled "special education" but who are not so disabled that they cannot work in the same classroom with others. Mainstreaming has had a bumpy ride in the past few years. Some teachers rail against it because they find themselves struggling with children who need a great deal of attention, even when they have paraprofessional aides in the classroom.

On the other hand, many teachers seem to have adjusted to mainstreaming well, because there are fewer angry discussions about it than formerly. It is possible that teachers have realized that the students' "disabilities" were manageable in classrooms that challenged them and left less time for distraction. Teachers have also been helped by workshops providing information on such problems as dyslexia, which can be baffling: how can a teacher help a child who sees letters reversed—*b* is always *d,* for example?

Mainstreaming has enormous advantages for students: students are not stigmatized by being assigned to different classes; they learn the same things as other, "normal" students; they have the same chances to excel. There is no doubt that mainstreaming presents challenges for teachers, especially those in school districts where there is no money for classroom paraprofessional aides. But there is no professional reward so great as seeing a student who seemed to have an insurmountable disability overcome it and achieve. One teacher told us recently about one of his students who seemed "slow" and needed special help: he followed the boy's progress into middle school, where he became class president in the eighth grade.

"Gifted and Talented"

Gifted and talented (GT) programs are another form of "special education," in this case special for those who apparently learn more quickly than others. GT programs skim the most highly motivated students into an academic elite where high expectations produce high results. In 1994, 6 percent of U.S. students were enrolled in gifted and talented programs. Eight states enrolled 10 percent or more, with Ohio leading the country by claiming an incredible 15 percent of its students as gifted.[52]

It's difficult to argue that this many children are truly gifted. Data collected by the Office of Civil Rights certainly raises the suspicion that gifted enrollments are padded with the high-achieving children of privileged families. In 1994, African-American students composed 17 percent of public school enrollments. Yet GT programs enrolled less than half that number. Nearly 79 percent of all GT students were white, even though they represented only 65 percent of public school students.[53] These inequities lead to the often-made charge that gifted programs are nothing but segregated private schools in a public school setting.

The GT category has a devastating effect in some school districts, where students who are tested and receive the designation are pulled from their neighborhood schools into special schools. The schools these students leave feel abandoned by their best students. In order to keep them in the school, they provide pull-out programs for GT students. Unfortunately these are often a hodgepodge of poorly designed programs intended to keep GT students from getting bored and therefore disruptive in their regular classes. Some students don't even go to the GT classes because they prefer to stay with their friends.

A standards-based system has an answer for GT students: if they have completed classwork for that grade, let them go ahead into the next higher grade. As we have said, students will meet standards in their own time, and this means that some students will need less, not more, time to do so.

Furthermore, every time we are shown exciting learning opportunities for the GT students, we ask: "Why don't all students have this program (or apparatus or computer program)?" What is good for GT students is good for all.

Good Teaching and High Expectations Make Good Students

A recent study of Minnesota middle-schoolers makes a convincing case for educating all students as GT students. Researchers looked at an apparent anomaly. While the state's eighth-graders put in the same lackluster performance as their U.S. peers in international assessments of mathematics, Minnesota's performance in science was far ahead of national average and, internationally, was exceeded only by Singapore.

The first findings from the study show the effects of good teaching: in science, Minnesota has high expectations for all students from elementary school on—all students, special and GT alike. This is not true in mathematics, where students are rigidly tracked with different content for different students.[54]

The Minnesota study confirms what several reports on the effects of tracking and ability grouping have been saying for more than a decade: children will rise to the expectations schools hold for them. High expectations are central to a standards-based system. When standards are linked to assessments and accountability, the community knows that all students, not just some, will be given access to rigorous and challenging subject matter.

In the next chapter, we show how two schools took very different approaches to literacy development and reached the same standards.

NOTES

1. Hodgkinson, "Reform Versus Reality," 8–16.

2. Quality Education for Minorities Project, *Education That Works*, 11.

3. Committee for Economic Development, *Unfinished Agenda*, 8.

4. U.S. Department of Education, "Entering Kindergarten."

5. Ibid., fig. 10, 11.

6. Ibid., fig. 1, 2.

7. Ibid., 5.

8. Ibid., fig. 9.

9. National Center for Education Statistics, NAEP *1998 Reading Report*, 19, 136, 139.

10. Education Trust, *Education Watch 1998*, vol. II.

11. National Center for Education Statistics, *Raising Standards for American Education*, 4.

12. Ibid., 10.

13. Benning, "Virginia School Overshoots Goal," B1. This account is drawn from Benning's article.

14. U.S. Department of Education, "Entering Kindergarten," 6.

15. *Education Watch 1998*, vol. II. 8.

16. U.S. Department of Education, *1996 National Mathematics Results*.

17. Resnick, *Education and Learning to Think*, 8.

18. Their research is reported in Newmann and Associates *Authentic Achievement, Restructuring Schools for Intellectual Quality* and is applied to a specific school district in Newmann, Lopez, and Bryk, *Quality of Intellectual Work in Chicago Schools*.

19. Newmann, Lopez, and Bryk, *Quality of Intellectual Work in Chicago Schools*, 12.

20. Ravitch, "Tot Sociology," (*American Scholar* 56, no. 3 [1987]: 343–354).

21. While there are many problems with the Virginia tests for social studies, the standards themselves, once revised, turned out to be fairly good.

22. Egan, *Teaching as Story Telling*, 62.

23. That she might be teaching at the middle or high school level is by no means impossible. We have examples of coloring and poster making at both.

24. Ferguson, "Paying for Public Education."

25. Hanushek, "Trade-off Between Child Quantity and Quality."

26. Haycock, "Good Teaching Matters," 4. Also see this paper for summaries of the Tennessee and Dallas research.

27. Johnson, *Hope for Urban Schools*.

28. Grissmer, Flanagan, and Flanagan, "Rapid Gains in North Carolina and Texas."

29. U.S. Department of Education, *Condition of Education, 2000*, table 47-2. In 1998 only 22 percent of elementary teachers had degrees in an academic field.

30. A brief but trenchant criticism of elementary teacher training can be found in Haberman, "Thirty-One Reasons to Stop the School Reading Machine," especially reasons twenty-one through twenty-four. Haberman is a professor of education at the University of Wisconsin–Milwaukee, and a credible critic of teacher education.

31. Farnham-Diggory, *Schooling*, 56.

32. Barth and Mitchell, "Not Good Enough."

33. Haycock, "*Good Teaching Matters.*"

34. Ferguson, "Can Schools Narrow the Black-White Test Score Gap?"

35. King, "Real Kids or Unreal Tasks," 6–9.

36. We have developed a professional development program called Standards in Practice (SIP), which has six steps, beginning with the

teacher's assignment and ending with action plans for revising or re-placing it.

37. Hollingsworth and Ybarra, *Analyzing Classroom Instruction,* 2.

38. Ibid., 3.

39. Fletcher and Lyon, "Reading: A Research-Based Approach," 51.

40. Ibid.

41. This conclusion was reached in 1985 in the U.S. Department of Education's *Becoming a Nation of Readers,* after a distinguished panel of experts looked at the evidence. It would be depressing to think that we need to go through this war and reconciliation cycle every decade!

42. Project 2061 of the American Association for the Advancement of Science had produced a report on what knowledge and skills were needed to be scientifically literate in 1986. "Science for All Americans" did not specifically define expectations at various grade levels, however. Since then, Project 2061 has published "Benchmarks" for science literacy, which greatly influenced the national science standards from the National Research Council as well a several state standards documents.

43. Leinwand, "It's Time to Abandon Computational Algorithms."

44. U.S. Department of Education, *National Assessment of Education Progress,* "Long-Term Trends in Student Mathematics Performance." Based on results since 1973, math achievement is improved for all age groups and subgroups, including blacks and Hispanics.

45. Gardner, *Frames of Mind.*

46. Many multiple intelligences web pages have sprung up. Gardner's own web page can be found at *www.pzweb.harvard.edu.*

47. This lesson was adapted from *The Midas News,* edited by Clifford Morris. This site, which showed over 60,000 hits, is located at *www.angelfire.com/oh/themidasnews/oct4art.html.* At this writing, there are conservatively over 1,000 websites devoted to multiple intelligences.

48. Gardner, *Intelligence Reframed.*

49. Success for All was developed at Johns Hopkins University in Baltimore. It is now run as a separate, nonprofit enterprise.

50. Adapted from Slavin, *Ability Grouping and Student Achievement in Elementary Schools.*

51. U.S. Department of Education, *Digest of Education Statistics, 1999,* 66.

52. Ibid.

53. Education Trust, *Education Watch, 1998,* vol. II, 31.

54. Barth et al., *Minnesota and TIMSS.*

CHAPTER FIVE

ALL
ROADS
LEAD
TO ROME

ELEMENTARY SCHOOL is no longer mostly about social adjustment and ensuring that children's self-esteem is nurtured. It is now about academic results. Children must learn to read and compute, and adults must be accountable for seeing that they do so. Does this seem harsh in comparison to the remembered cozy atmosphere of elementary schools? It should not, as we shall demonstrate with descriptions of two schools where children are successful. In these schools, self-esteem comes from success in being able to read, write correctly, answer adults clearly and confidently, and work well both alone and in groups. The atmosphere is cozy, if cozy means calm, focused, cheerful, and busy.

These schools are different from each other—and that's the point. A mistaken notion about standards is that it leads to standardized education, that all students will be on the same page on the same day. But, as we have repeated throughout this book, standards do not tell schools HOW students should learn, only WHAT they should learn and how well.

This means that schools can adopt any number of approaches to achieving the standards. We are frequently asked what works best to teach reading to elementary students, especially poor and minority students. People seem to want us to advocate specific programs—Success for All, Reading Recovery, Guided Reading—but our experience has shown us that different programs work differently in various contexts. For each of these programs and for the ones we shall describe in detail, there are stories of success on standardized tests and stories of failure. Success seems to depend on a good match between the teachers and the features of the programs, thorough training, school leadership that supports the program, and early evidence that the program is succeeding. We do not advocate one program over another, but we do advocate looking at a number of literacy programs and asking if they fit with the student body, the teachers, and the administration. If it works—if the students can read and write confidently—then that program is right for this school at this time.

To illustrate the point, we're going to describe two schools that are equally successful in enabling children to read and score well on standardized tests, but they have different approaches. In fact, our first school rejected Direct Instruction, the program embraced by the second school, after having used the method for several years.

A LITERACY MODEL GROWS IN BROOKLYN

"Okay, everyone to your book bin."

The second-graders scurry to the corner where rows of colorful plastic baskets are kept, each marked with a student's name. Each basket contains two to three books personally selected by its owner. The children pick one out, return to their seats, and start reading. It is May. At this point in the school year, they know the routine and are well on their way to completing their required twenty-five books.

"Shanice, Sam, Irena, and Carlos, join me on the reading rug." Four children hear their names and move to the carpeted square, where they plop down and open their books. One at a time they read aloud quietly to the teacher, who sits cross-legged next to them. While she listens, she takes careful notes:

Sam: good articulation—repeats "Howie."

"The two dogs trampled Mr. Puffin's roses and tore up his sssst … sstuh …" *stops on "stocks."*

"Think of another word like this," she coaches.

"Hmmm … clocks, ssstocks."

"Do you know what stocks are?"

Sam shakes his head. "Flowers?"

"That's right. Go on."

The teacher records: *uses context clues.*

From the streets outside, sirens interrupt the quiet. But the children at their tables are not distracted by the noise, so absorbed are they in their reading. Most of them are reading chapter books. *Junie B. Jones* is a popular choice. But a few prefer science books. A boy in a Yankees cap leaves his seat to add the word *bellicose* to the class list of Words to Look Up. Two students are reading *Alice in Wonderland,* abridged in length, but not in style. Lewis Carroll's nineteenth-century words still resonate on the pages.

A group of three students huddles around another teacher, or is it a parent? It's hard to tell because so many adults move freely in and out of classrooms in this school. She is asking the children about the book they are reading together, *The Puppy Who Wanted a Boy.* It's clear that her questioning is intended to build their comprehension. They will write about the story in the writing workshop later that day.

This Brooklyn elementary school serves a diverse student population in a progressive community. The principal affectionately describes her educated parents as "former hippies." About half the enrollment is white; the rest are African American, Latino, and Asian. The school's families are Jewish, Christian, and Muslim. One in four students qualify for subsidized lunches, low by New York City standards, but high compared to suburban schools. This is not a wealthy community; the families are mostly middle class.

The school is huge, about the size of many high schools. It enrolls over 1,200 students, prekindergarten through grade 5. But it doesn't feel like the overly large, impersonal institution it easily could be, and it's hard to imagine any child here falling through the cracks. Creative scheduling by administrators helps by keeping class size reasonable: an average of twenty-five students. Most important, the school has a history of building a feeling of community throughout the school. The current principal and faculty are maintaining a long tradition in the school that values learning among children and adults alike.

High expectations are also evident. The heterogeneously grouped classrooms contain students who in other schools would be segregated into gifted or special-ed tracks. The results are impressive: the school is a consistently high performer in its district. And, remarkable for an urban neighborhood school, it ranks in the state's top quartile in reading and mathematics.

Writing to Read, Reading to Write

Twenty years ago this elementary school made a commitment to develop literacy through reading and writing processes. It entered into a close collaboration with the Teachers' College Reading and Writing Project at nearby Columbia University, which continues to this day. In the summer months, new and veteran teachers receive intensive training in new approaches to teaching language arts. During the school year they have regularly scheduled time to design curriculum and discuss problems with their colleagues. The faculty is continuously learning so their students can learn to marshal language to make sense of the world. The school has transformed, in their words, into a "community of writers."

The emphasis strikes visitors as soon as they enter the doors. The office and corridor walls devoted to children's artwork in most schools are instead filled with pages of students' written words. We visited during Poetry Month, and students' poems dominated the bulletin boards. The principal told us that this annual event was a reward for the children after a year's hard work. All of the children will be able to publish their work in *Pandemonium,* the poetry magazine sponsored and distributed by the school's parent organization.

The school's philosophy is not merely writing for its own sake. New York City has adopted the *New Standards Performance Standards* (among the documents that influenced our list in chapter three), which ask for various kinds of writing besides stories and poems. In addition to the poetry, we saw plenty of examples of student writing that were intended to communicate how well students read, listen, and think. The bulletin board outside the third-grade classrooms, for example, featured the children's responses to a lesson in art criticism, which we found challenging ourselves. These New York eight-year-olds had completed a curriculum unit on van Gogh that combined readings and teacher lecture, culminating in the enviable opportunity to view an exhibit of the Dutch painter's work at the Metropolitan Museum. For their final assignment, pictures of van Gogh paintings were each paired with a painting by another Impressionist artist, but the artists' names were concealed. The students were asked to identify the van Gogh in the pair and explain their choice in writing. Their responses were scored on how well they used evidence found in the text—in this case, paintings—to show what they understood about van Gogh's art in particular and Impressionism in general.

The responses were quite sophisticated. The children discussed and compared such characteristics as color, brush strokes, and subject matter in the paintings. It was by no means straightforward. We thought the lesson was an excellent way to develop students' power of observation, their ability to analyze what they see, and their skill at communicating their ideas clearly—skills that are also important in science writing.

In this school, the text is central; skills are developed within the context of language and comprehension. The school culture encourages the free exchange of ideas and taking intellectual risks. It all springs from the words on the page, the brush strokes on the canvas, the phrases from the speaker's mouth. Stories and articles are read, then discussed in groups; students independently write about a question raised in the discussion; the writing is discussed by peers and then goes back to the writer to be revised for content, edited for mechanics, and submitted for a grade. Rubrics posted around the classroom inform each step of the process, including standards for discussion that the students practice from the time they're in kindergarten: listen respectfully, refer to the comments of other speakers, refer to the text. The cycle is so well integrated it's impossible to separate the pieces from the whole.

The principal calls this a "model literacy school." One could call it a whole language school and not be totally wrong. Kindergartners begin "writing" on their first day—typically before they are reading on their own. At this age, the work that qualifies as writing is mostly drawing, but the habit is established. The children participate in writing workshops several times a week where they are encouraged to put their ideas or stories on paper. Over the course of the year, the drawings evolve. At some point children begin to add "words," which typically constitute beginning consonants. An adult or older student coach will supply the translation, writing the actual words underneath the child's letters. Slowly more consonants are added, and later, vowels.

These invented or "temporary" spellings are indulged in kindergarten and first grade in order to encourage children to use vocabulary in writing that they understand but don't know how to spell. However, the children are aware that there are correct spellings for words that may not be the same as the ones they put on paper. There is no anxiety at the sight of the teacher's red pencil when children know they are learning from the correction and not being penalized for something they have not been taught. Explicit spelling instruction is part of program, and by the end of first grade, students will be expected to correctly spell the words from these lessons in their final drafts. In the meantime their practice with writing words, correctly spelled or not, is laying the foundation for reading them.

Learning to read, therefore, is a seamless part of the whole experience with language, along with writing and discussion. "Word study," which includes vocabulary, phonics, and spelling, is taught in the writing workshop as well as in discrete mini-lessons, depending in large part on teachers' preferences and the needs of the students. Teachers at all grade levels read to their classes. In the early grades teachers read out of oversized picture books so that children can follow along with the text. There is also time each day for independent reading and small-group work with a teacher, as in the scene we described earlier, or just with other students. And the cycle is set in motion. Stories are read and then discussed in small groups or as a whole class, which leads again to writing.

Accountable Talk

We entered a fourth-grade class as the teacher was beginning to read to the students. The novel was about an adolescent girl who was in the foster care of an elderly woman. The teacher read with great drama, and we suspected he began his career with acting ambitions. The chapter was filled with dialogue, and he effectively mimicked the voices of the old woman and the much younger girl. There was conflict. The girl resented the foster parent for keeping her away from her real mother—or so she thought. The reader conveyed all the tension with just the right modulations of his voice.

It didn't surprise us, then, that he was able to hold the class of twenty-seven in such rapt attention. The teacher read from a chair at the

head of the circle of students packed shoulder to shoulder in chairs. A handful were crowded on the couch at the southern edge of the fourth-grade "reading rug." They were completely silent.

Then he stopped reading. And what followed next surprised us a great deal. He shut the book, glanced up, and noiselessly the students slipped from their chairs to the floor. With no signal that we could discern the students began one at a time to comment on the motivations of the young heroine. Were they picking up on questions they had been discussing every day? We didn't know. But there was nothing in the teacher's behavior to suggest that it was anything but spontaneous. The children politely allowed others to finish their points before making their own. As the discussion progressed, the students would often make reference to the comments already made by their peers. They would either elaborate further or disagree, but they always cited the text for support.

The teacher was silent through most of it. With an almost imperceptible nod or wave of his hand he would pull shy students into the discussion or subdue someone trying to dominate. He intervened only once. Two students had begun to explore a different angle to the character but allowed the point to drift off. Speaking for the first time, the teacher asked the class to return to the connection the two students had noticed and attempt to dig into it deeper.

After about twenty minutes the teacher stopped the discussion. He instructed the students to think about the character and see if they could relate her experiences to their own. This would be the topic for their journal writing that day.

These children are practicing accountable talk, as expected in a school following the Institute for Learning's Principles of Learning.[1] Their comments are disciplined; they are focused completely on the topic. Again, the text is central. When they make an assertion they use evidence from the text to support their claim. They may draw connections from other works or experiences, but they always come back to the text. In the best discussions, there is no single right answer, but there are clearly wrong ones if it's not in the text. Unsupported opinions will not do.

Accountable talk has also taught these students a lesson that we adults often have trouble with. They have learned to negotiate the give and take of debate while always respecting other points of view. It's no accident that these children are so polite with each other. It comes from years of discussing ideas in an environment where every viewpoint is valued as a search for meaning and where students will be helped along in their struggle to find it. It is also an environment to which everyone contributes. Every child will be heard.

As marvelous as this teacher is, he could not do what he does so effectively in a school culture that did not support his educational philosophy. His students had been developing listening skills and internalizing the rules of discussion since they entered the kindergarten door for the first time in this school. They had experienced years of guided questions from their teachers, so they now have strategies to help them mine texts for ideas. The emphasis on reading, writing, and the critical engagement with texts of all kinds had further developed their capacity to think analytically. This teacher did not act alone.

This "model literacy school" succeeds because it has institutionalized an infrastructure that supports teachers' learning alongside student learning, earning it a reputation as a good place to work. The school attracts applications from the best teacher colleges in the region, so the principal has the luxury of picking and choosing among the very best. She further benefits from a community that endorses the school's progressive approach. It's a combination that consistently produces students who meet the highest standards.

DIRECT INSTRUCTION IN HOUSTON

The school is fenced in wrought iron. The fence is symbolic as well as functional. It divides the extensive school grounds and the clean, freshly painted buildings from the almost rural poverty of the houses around it. This is inner-city Houston, where African Americans live in tiny individual houses facing narrow roads with no sidewalks. The dense greenness of the vegetation provides a moist shade over the abandoned cars in overgrown driveways. Freeways connect these neighborhoods to downtown, but they also isolate them. This would be an enclave of hopelessness without its schools.

The elementary schools in this community are doing well on the Texas Assessment of Academic Skills (TAAS), the statewide test that assesses progress in reading, writing, and mathematics throughout elementary school and must be passed for graduation from high school. The distinguishing feature of TAAS is its reporting: the scores are not reported as averages for a school, but by the groups making up the school population—African Americans, Hispanics, whites, Asians—including poor children eligible for federal Title 1 assistance. All these groups must achieve a high percentage of correct answers on TAAS for the school to attain Recognized or Exemplary status; if it falls below a certain percentage, the school is liable for sanctions.

The school we are entering at 8:30 in the morning is a Recognized school according to this year's TAAS scores.[2] It is a large school—850 students, almost all African American, 82 percent eligible for Title 1, grades K–5—although not as large as the Brooklyn school we visited. (Both, we believe, are too large for elementary schools.)

In the broad corridor we notice that there is a teacher standing quietly at the open door of each classroom. At a signal, students file in from the playground to the classrooms, where the teacher greets them as they enter; after the last student has walked in with arms crossed over the chest, the chanting begins. Up and down the corridor children are shouting in unison: the alphabet forward and backward, numbers to 100, numbers by tens and fives to 100, names of states as the teacher points to them, names of countries on a globe. We are in a corridor of kindergarten and first-grade classes.

A little while later, when the chanting has ended and the corridor is quiet except for the rustle of students moving into reading groups in each classroom, we enter a kindergarten class. A circle of children is sitting around the teacher, holding books above their laps. Another group of children is on the floor, sharing large crayons while they color an illustration. One or two children are sitting at desks, their fingers pointing to the pages in front of them as they murmur the words to themselves.

The teacher has a book from which she is reading. It is spiral-bound at the top so that she turns it over as she proceeds through the lesson. The book is a complete script for each lesson: what the teacher must say, what the children must do, the text of the book they are reading, the questions to be asked—all are in the script.

The children put their index fingers on the page and read together. The teacher asks them questions about the action in the narrative: "What did the cowboy do then?" "What happened to his horse?" The children answer, individually or in unison. They read individually, although the teacher occasionally has to remind the others in the reading group that they must pay attention to the reader and not squirm around to look at the visitors. Some children have to be reminded to sit straight in their chairs and put their feet on the floor. The feet are covered in what used to be called sensible shoes: this school has a uniform, so bare feet in sandals and baseball caps are not seen here.

The group we are watching is a group of good readers, students who have less difficulty than their peers in grasping the skill of reading. Direct Instruction does not track, but it uses ability grouping so that students with a similar skill level are working together. These are temporary groups. Every five lessons the script includes a mastery test, so that students have frequent opportunities to be regrouped.

When the readers come to words they don't know, they sound them out phonetically. They have obviously learned phonics, but at the beginning of the school year and simultaneously with reading text. It is now April and phonics instruction is incorporated into reading.

Everything in Direct Instruction is done at speed. Teachers beat time as students chant, and they urge students along as they read and respond. The speed has several advantages: it keeps the attention of students used to the flashing speed of television images, it ensures that there are no long pauses when children can get bored and look around for entertainment—which means getting into trouble in many cases, and it helps students to grasp the meaning of what they read, as decoding alone can be so laborious that meaning is lost. Reading slowly is a sure sign of incomprehension.

Everything is also repeated, again and again, and with a strong rhythm to the chanting. This chanting makes noise legitimate and incorporates it into the learning process. So by using speed, repetition, and noisy chanting, Direct Instruction aligns school with the students' experiences and channels them productively instead of fighting them by demanding that students pay silent attention to boring material.

Clear evidence of the effectiveness of speed, repetition, and acceptable noise came when we asked the school's nurse how many children received Ritalin daily. Ritalin is a drug used to calm the hyperactivity of children diagnosed as suffering from attention deficit-hyperactivity disorder. In many elementary schools the line of children (mostly boys, often African American) waiting outside the nurse's office is a regular feature of the school day. Nationally, as many as 5 percent of school-age children are estimated to be on Ritalin or similar drugs. In some schools, it's much higher.

In this Houston school where there are 850 students, only one student was on Ritalin and a few others (fewer than ten) had been prescribed a similar drug. In addition, there were almost no special education students beyond the ones with obvious physical disabilities—no dyslexics or severe behavioral problems.

Reading and Understanding

So the students were actively engaged, focused on their tasks. Were they reading and understanding what they read?

After we had watched the reading group for a while, they changed configurations so that the group on the floor went to the reading corner and the others clustered around us to read to us. The competition was so fierce to read to us that we had to ask them to form a line to take turns. As LaTanya read, we stopped her and asked about the words she was reading. "What's a hound?" "A dog," she answered with a faint trace of contempt for my ignorance. It was obvious that she understood the story and was not repeating from memory. She made none of the mistakes that memory causes: she did not read *dog* for *hound* as she might have done if remembering the story.

All the kindergartners could read the text "leveled" for them and could answer questions about the story and the motivations of the characters. They also knew where the continents are on a map of the world and could connect every state with its capital. We stumped them, though, when we told them we were from Washington, D.C.—not surprisingly, because many adults do not know that Washington is not part of any state. They soon learned where it is, so another visitor from the nation's capital won't get blank stares.

In the first grade we watched a teacher with a group that was rated slower to learn to read than the kindergarten children. She used repetition and chanting with them to understand word families (these are words that differ only in one phoneme, such as *cat, bat, rat*, or inflected words such as *read, reading, reader*) and urged them along with her obvious energy.

In the fifth grade we watched a social studies class reading about imports and exports. The textbook was one of the Direct Instruction publications now available through a commercial publisher. It was dense with text and did not have the flashy pictures and jazzy design of most comparable fifth-grade social studies texts. But the students were intent on it, reading sophisticated information about international markets, and asking probing questions in complete sentences. One fifth-grader asked, "If Toyotas are made in this country, are they imported cars? Are they Japanese or American?" He spoke confidently and clearly. The discussion proceeded through legal definitions, consequences for taxes and import duties, and the market for imported cars.

The evidence was overwhelming that children were reading and understanding what they read. In most classes, children were divided into two or three groups, with some working quietly at their desks, reading or writing, while others met in groups with the teacher, and in some cases with an aide or additional teacher (it could be a trainee, as we were told afterward). No children were disengaged, wandering around the room, or sleeping at their desks. Whenever asked, children answered confidently, described their reading or writing, and seemed proud of their abilities.

The Script

Direct Instruction (DI), the method that gets students reading in kindergarten and never stopping from there on, is not much loved in the education community. Developed by Siegfried Engelmann in the 1960s (when it was called Direct Instruction System for Teaching Arithmetic and Reading, or DISTAR), it is regarded by some as demeaning to students and teachers alike because so much of it is scripted.[3] Some people think of DI as training children to behave like circus animals, performing on command. As we mentioned earlier, the school in the first of these two portraits rejected DI and adopted Literacy Institute principles.

In the 1970s the U.S. Department of Education conducted a study over a number of years to evaluate the effectiveness of various curriculums in elementary education.[4] DI came out first, ahead of such programs as Cognitive Oriented Curriculum, Responsive Education, and the Bank Street College model. DI produced higher gains for students in language, mathematics computation and problem solving, and reading comprehension. Ironically, the DI students also scored highest in measures of self-esteem. The news was not received well and as far as possible was suppressed, so when people are told the story now, they are surprised.

The major objection to the DI method was its dependence on that script we saw in every teacher's hands, the script that dictates every move and word. Teachers and teacher educators in university teacher preparation institutions objected to the script because it eliminated the teacher's creativity. They called it teacher-proofing, a condemnation in their eyes because it reduced the teacher to an automaton who could put no personal imprint on teaching.

The standards movement and its insistence that all children learn to read and write early has revived interest in DI. School districts faced with massive failures among low-income and minority populations, failures made glaringly clear in the light of accountability measures such as TAAS, have adopted DI precisely because it has a script.

The script, like it or not, incorporates recognized methods of teaching children to read. As we said in chapter four, far too many teachers emerge from teacher preparation institutions without specific training in subject matter or in teaching reading. If teachers are well trained and talented in techniques of teaching reading, they justifiably can work without a script. But if they have not received good training, then using a script is a great deal better than stumbling through on scraps of knowledge and good intentions.

Furthermore, the questions included in the script are precisely those that a good teacher of reading comprehension would ask. When teachers use the script, they are asking students in inner-city schools the same questions that well-trained teachers in the suburbs are asking their students. *In other words, accountable talk is built into the script.*[5]

That this works and has lasting effects was exemplified by our experience in the fifth-grade social studies class in the same school. The habit of thinking about reading was clear from the ease with which these students could ask questions and discuss the topic.

Not a Panacea

In education there are no silver bullets, a fact that many superintendents and school district administrators desperately wish were not true. DI is not a panacea, but it is a viable option for ensuring that some populations of students learn to read easily and well.

In some schools, such as those in Houston, DI is the curriculum. Entering another school in the same neighborhood, we heard the familiar chanting resounding from an open door. In this school we were introduced to a young Hispanic student in a first-grade writing class who proudly showed us how he could write in English. In such schools, literacy and arithmetic take up the whole morning, and the afternoons are devoted to history, art, and science, all treated as opportunities to further practice literacy skills. Many schools that adopt the DI curriculum also extend their day so that students have an additional hour in the afternoon to work on literacy.[6]

Other schools use DI materials as part, but not all, of their curriculum. Many of them have the same spectacular success in getting students to read early. But DI materials in themselves do not guarantee success for all children. We have seen DI materials used where teachers could not control reading groups. Some teachers do not follow the script exactly, and the continuity is lost.

Nevertheless, where certain other ingredients of success are in place, using DI materials with other ingredients works well. What are those other ingredients? Committed, knowledgeable leadership, usually a principal with the passion and energy of ten ordinary people who continuously monitors what goes on in classrooms. Professional development for teachers, regularly built into their schedule. Opportunity for teachers to work together professionally so that they can bolster each other with solutions to the problems posed by students. Above all, a sharp focus on academic achievement attainable by these students is shared by everyone connected with the school, from the principal through to the teachers, the parents, the office and cafeteria staff, to the crossing guard.

WHATEVER WORKS

We have described two contrasting approaches to literacy, the major focus of the elementary school. If elementary school does not produce students who can read and write easily across a wide range of subject matter, it has failed. This has always been the case, but standards and accountability have made it manifest to public view.

But we cannot say honestly that the approach to literacy followed in our first school is universally better than DI, or vice versa. The circumstances surrounding each school and the choice they made affect the success of the method.

The first school is located in a neighborhood of great ethnic diversity, although all groups seem to share the great New York characteristic of loving to talk, and talking a lot. This means that students are used to talking when they come to the school, and talking is therefore a way into literacy for these students.

The Houston school is largely African American, also a verbal culture, but more concerned with the expression of emotions than dialogue.[7] For them and other students who may have had little exposure to print in their homes, expanding vocabulary through contact with print sparks students' curiosity and excites them with the possibilities of something new and strange, but is delivered in the familiar form of rhythmic chanting.

The Brooklyn school also has well-trained teachers who understand how to teach reading. The school's reputation attracts teachers so that the principal can choose among candidates. They rarely leave except for promotions. In addition, the school provides ongoing and intense professional development: there are full-time staff developers whose job it is to provide assistance to the others, with weekly meetings and consultation available at other times.

Many schools that choose DI do not have the luxury of choice when they hire teachers. This is not to despise them or to denigrate them in any way. Teachers with good training and reputation can earn more in suburban schools than in the inner city, and in their eyes the conditions of work are more congenial. Given that most principals in inner-city schools may not be able to employ teachers who know how to teach reading and how to diagnose and treat reading difficulties, they may decide that a scripted curriculum is the best choice.

And there is always the issue of personality—the personality of the principal and of the teachers, as well as the cultural expectations of the students that we have alluded to. Parents' attitudes toward school and their level of participation are also factors. All these go into the mix.

In the main, the choice is between a heavily scripted program and one that guides teachers but does not dictate their every move. Direct Instruction is not the only scripted program for literacy; Success for All is another example. And even Literacy in Action, a program similar to the Institute for Learning's Literacy Institute, includes directions for the organization of a classroom for literacy experiences and for questions that should be asked of readers and writers.

No one outside the school community can make the choice for them. The objective is literacy for all the students—reading at first grade, confident reading and writing across the curriculum at sixth grade. It may be that a program will work, or parts of several programs. If the children are successful in reaching the standards, it works.

NOTES

1. Developed by Lauren Resnick and her associates at the Learning Research and Development Center at the University of Pittsburgh and a feature of professional development offered by the New Standards Project (see chapter three, note 5, page 47).

2. The four levels of achievement are Exemplary, Recognized, Acceptable, and Low Performing.

3. Dr. Engelmann is now at the University of Oregon in Eugene, Oregon. Direct Instruction materials are available from SRI International.

4. Project Follow Through, as it was called then; 1968–1977, funded by the U.S. Office of Economic Opportunity and the U.S. Office of Education. A recent survey by the American Institutes for Research showed that DI was one of only three reform models to show evidence of strong positive effects on student achievement (*Educator's Guide to Schoolwide Reform*, 5).

5. We are indebted to our colleague Dr. Stephanie Robinson for this insight.

6. An elementary school in Cincinnati, Ohio, adopted this plan. The principal employed only teachers who would agree to the extended hours. In two years, this elementary school has moved from the lowest of Cincinnati Public Schools' four accountability classifications, Redesign, to the highest, Achievement.

7. The contrasts among the verbal characteristics of three cultures was explored in Shirley Brice Heath's "What No Bedtime Story Means," summarized in the first edition of *Smart Start*, 33.

CHAPTER SIX

PREPARING FOR A TECHNOLOGICAL WORLD

A S THE 1990S began, the fax machine was the big advance in office communications (how many now remember that *fax* is short for *facsimile?*), and a few of us were buying our first home computers. CD-ROM and the Internet were unknown to most Americans. Computers were beginning to appear in schools, but their use was limited to word processing and occasional drill and practice. Cutting-edge technology in schools usually meant calculators, video cameras, and cable TV.

At the onset of the new millennium, nearly half of our households have computers and half of them are linked to the Internet.[1] Computers and digital technology are ubiquitous in the workplace. They are central to every job from general office work to manufacturing jobs to cashiering. Nearly every school now has computers with Internet access.[2] Interactive software provides virtual coaches in every subject. Distance learning brings students in touch with working scientists from places as remote as Antarctica and just beyond Earth's atmosphere.

Computer technology gives students the ability to accelerate their learning and extend their understanding into areas not possible without it. By removing the tedium from paper-and-pencil computations, for example, calculators and electronic spreadsheets allow even young children to conduct databased projects that would have been prohibitively laborious by hand. Elementary students are further able to explore new domains of mathematics, such as discrete mathematics and combinatorics, which were known to only a handful of mathematicians in the precomputer age. A few key scientific concepts, such as why there are phases of the Moon, have typically bedeviled students' understanding because they seem counterintuitive to what we actually see. Computer simulations not only make these concepts instantly understandable, they make knowledge accessible to children at an earlier age than imagined not too long ago.

Technology can also break down the walls that cut off so many schools from the rest of the world. Students sitting in remote rural communities or inner-city isolation can nonetheless link to NASA databases, the National Weather Service, and many agencies worldwide that open their resources to classrooms for conducting real research. Where qualified teachers are scarce, on-line courses can provide expertise in notoriously hard-to-fill subjects such as mathematics and science. Teachers and students can share ideas and seek the advice of peers by communicating through e-mail, message boards, and chat rooms.

Given its great potential, it's not surprising that technology appears on the education reform agendas of many groups and interests. Business leaders demand technological literacy in the workforce as much as mathematical and verbal skills, and they expect schools to prepare graduates accordingly. Educators, parents, and policy makers place computers high on their list of necessary educational resources. Providing technology to schools is a favorite for corporate givers.

Many states and districts are making huge investments in equipping classrooms with computers and adding phone lines to link them to the Internet. But while communities support putting computers in classrooms, they aren't as clear about the results this investment is supposed to produce. Is it hoped that students will learn how to use the technology? Do communities expect student achievement to increase because of technology? Or are they merely reacting to a vague perception that their students need computers so they can compete with other students who have them?

There are many good reasons to invest in technology. But the confusion about outcomes has led many communities to think that once they put computers in schools their job is done. They can now sit back and wait for good things to happen, whatever they are. But too often districts have not provided enough training for teachers or designed schedules that would give students and teachers enough time with the new technology. A chronic complaint from teachers is the lack of technical support just to maintain the equipment. Despite all its promise, computer technology has yet to fundamentally change instruction in our schools.

Using new technologies effectively requires districts to first decide on the outcome. As we have argued throughout this book, the primary mission of elementary school is the academic preparation of students so they will be ready for the work of middle school. Everything that happens in the classroom should be aligned with this goal. Technology is no exception.

WHY NO TECHNOLOGY STANDARDS?

Given the importance of technology to functioning in today's world, readers might be wondering if we shouldn't have standards for technology alongside the other subjects. In fact, many such standards exist. Several states and districts have drafted technology standards, and national models are available, notably from the International Society for Technology in Education.

The documents generally emphasize knowing how to use technology. This is not an academic objective. Seen properly, technology is a tool for learning. While using it effectively implies proficiency in handling the tool, the use itself is not the ultimate goal. Technology, like curriculum, should be in service of academic standards. Making technology equal to academics is yet another distraction from the core mission of schools.

There's an even more practical reason for not having technology standards. We have witnessed profound technological revolutions that, in a short time span, have replaced everything that went before. Standards for using present technology could easily be obsolete in a few years. What, then, have students gained?

We once visited a vocational school where students were being taught welding with equipment and methods that had not been used in the field for a decade. After two years in the program, students had learned how to do something no one in the working world did anymore. It took another two years for these students to learn welding as it's really practiced. So it is with computer technology. The only thing we can anticipate for certain is that it will change. Children need to be prepared for whatever comes.

A far better approach to technology education is to teach students to adapt to new situations, to analyze what they need for a particular task, and to identify the tools that will work best to accomplish it. This means students need a firm grounding in mathematics, science, and the humanities and must have good problem-solving skills in addition to merely being able to navigate the computer keyboard.

Placing technology in service of standards should not diminish its importance to children's education, however. As a tool, computer technology is so powerful that students who don't have it, or don't know how to use it well if they do, are at a serious disadvantage.

THE DIGITAL DIVIDE

Access to information in today's world can be a great leveler of opportunity. Sitting at our computers we can conduct our finances, earn college credits, get a job, buy a car, advocate for a cause, and join a community of people who share our hobbies and interests. For many young people the hours spent working and playing with computers ultimately lead to lucrative careers in website design, systems administration, programming, and the new IT fields that seem to pop up daily. Computers put us in touch with the information we need in order to find our way to the places we want to be. Sometimes they open up possibilities to us that we hadn't even imagined.

The fact that many people do not have this access drives an even deeper wedge between the haves and have-nots in our society. According to Commerce Department data, the digital divide between Americans isn't showing any signs of abating and is actually showing disturbing signs of widening. Affluent urban households are over twenty times as likely to have Internet access as low-income rural residents. Gaps also exist according to race: white and Asian households are over twice as likely to be on-line as either black or Hispanic homes.[3]

The school is the obvious place to make up for the resources children lack at home. And we have made considerable progress in getting schools hooked up to the Net. In 1999 over 90 percent of all schools—regardless of geographic location or the income level of the student population—had Internet access. In addition, since 1984 the gap in computer use at school has narrowed significantly between poor and more affluent students. Our youngest students are using a computer in school at least once a week— more than their older brothers and sisters in middle and high school. In addition, they now report using the computer "to learn things" as often as they use it to write or play games, whether at school or at home.

Despite these gains, important differences in access to technology remain. Even though schools are now on-line at about the same rates, Internet access is not equally available to all students. Those attending high-poverty schools have only half the chance to use the Internet in their classrooms, labs, or libraries as students in other schools.[4] Instead, the on-line computers in poor schools tend to be kept in offices where they're not available to students at all.

The deepest divide, however, is in access to technology outside of school. Home computers are still virtually unknown to our poorest children.[5] Anyone who has both a computer and kids at home has seen how adept young people become by spending hours playing and experimenting with the technology. For many children, the payoff in expertise is enormous.

We once met a charming fifth-grader from Kentucky who was the official techie for his school. His principal actually scheduled time during the school day for this boy to maintain all the school's computers. He told us he had been doing it since second grade. Clearly, he didn't learn how to do this in school. Such advantages come to children with a home computer and unlimited time. A weekly trip to the school's lab just isn't enough to compensate.

The divide also exists between the ways schools use the precious time they give children on computers. Some students get to use computers for more substantial work than others. Recent studies have shown that students who use computers for problem-solving tasks produce higher test scores than those who use them primarily for the discrete development of basic skills. Yet not all kids get the chance to use high-level applications. African-American children and children from low-income families are given far fewer chances than other students to use computers for simulations and applications. When poor and minority students are given computer time, it tends to be for drill and practice.[6]

The nation is making great strides in putting computers in schools. But we still have a lot of work to do to make sure they are used to extend student learning and not merely as glorified and expensive worksheets. Schools need to pay particular attention to the kind of computer experiences given to the children who don't have this resource available at home. If we can't close the digital divide during elementary school, we risk losing another generation to a life of dwindling expectations.

ENGAGING
THE DISENGAGED

In his book *Geeks,* Jon Katz describes a typical scene for two very bright, technologically literate young men who exemplify the techie personality. The boys are sitting at their computers. They simultaneously play an on-line computer game, download music, converse with a sister through instant messaging, eat lunch, conduct business by e-mail, print out play lists, and carry on a conversation with the author witnessing the flurry. Katz writes, "[They were] playing, working, networking, visiting, strategizing—all without skipping a function, getting confused, or stopping to think."[7]

The new technology is fast and furious. The desktop computer integrates the range of media to allow for the dizzying scene with the two boys above. This ability has spawned a new word: *multitasking,* doing several things at once. To those of us who predate the personal computer, the pace can be overwhelming.

Not so for today's children. They have been learning in a hyperstimulated world from the time they were babies. Author Thomas Armstrong writes, "These kids live life in the fast lane, and have evolved new ways of paying attention to cope with the increased pace."[8] While it would be foolish for schools to operate at the high velocity of MTV, the fact remains that the world outside school for many children is more intellectually interesting than the world inside. It shouldn't surprise, then, when some kids struggle in school. What should surprise is that more kids don't.

One of the powerful points made in Katz's book is that, despite their obvious (to him) talents, his adolescent heroes were both social and academic outcasts in school. For children like Andrew in chapter one, the estrangement from school begins early. Teachers see confusion and respond with more worksheets, more formulaic books, more drills that feature one isolated, single task at a time. Often these students are labeled with attention deficit disorder (ADD) or attention deficit-hyperactivity disorder (ADHD) and prescribed psychoactive drugs such as Ritalin to keep them focused. Armstrong again: "Children labeled ADD do most poorly in environments that are boring and repetitive, externally controlled, [or] lack immediate feedback. ... Unfortunately, this kind of classroom is deadly not only for the so-called ADD kid, but for all kids."[9]

Technology *is* interesting. Software gives children the stimulation that traditional teaching lacks. So-called living books allow emerging readers to read the story themselves; hear it read to them as they follow each word being pronounced; stop on unfamiliar words and be coached with phonetic or context clues, or hear the word pronounced. Plus they can animate the pictures. Children have complete control over how they interact with the text. Several popular mathematics programs set up sophisticated—and exciting—scenarios for students to exercise both basic math facts and problem-solving skills. Motivation for kids to ratchet up their skill level is a built-in feature. Even elementary students can be let loose to design the classroom web page, which brings together all kinds of skills. The new technology doesn't discourage multitasking, it demands it.

Computers in the classroom won't completely displace the value of reading real books, working with peers, or interacting with a teacher. But used well, they should have a much more central place than they currently occupy, especially for children for whom business as usual is getting them nowhere. For disengaged students, technology can provide the stimulation they need to get them reengaged in learning. It's certainly better for them than Ritalin.

Clearly, the world we are preparing our children for demands a different and higher level of knowledge and skill than life did before the microchip. The standards in chapter three acknowledge that this work must begin in elementary school. But while technology has raised the bar on what students need to learn, it also provides a vehicle for helping them succeed. In the rest of this chapter we discuss how specific technologies can be marvelous tools for moving schoolchildren to higher levels of learning.

CALCULATING

Interestingly, many of the same parents who insist on having computers in schools object to using calculators in mathematics class. Indeed, the flames of the math wars are stoked by parents' fear that calculators in the early grades will prevent children from learning the basics. On the other hand, the National Council of Teachers of Mathematics standards encourage the appropriate use of calculators to give students more opportunity to focus on problem solving and not get bogged down by tedious calculations. Of course, everyone wants the same thing: children who are mathematically proficient. The problem is defining what constitutes "appropriate use."

Survey data from the National Assessment of Education Progress (NAEP) highlights the relationship between calculator use and student achievement. Fourth-graders who report that they *occasionally* use calculators for math produce the highest NAEP scores compared to students who *never* use them and, interestingly, significantly better scores than those who report using calculators *every day*. By eighth grade, the relationship of daily use shifts. Eighth-graders who use calculators for tests *every day* scored the highest, and scored significantly higher than students who *never* use them. The difference between daily use and no use translates to more than one full grade level of achievement.[10]

The standards in chapter three assume that calculators will be introduced to young students as part of their math instruction. They also expect that children will internalize math facts. Remember our fourth guiding principle: Instruction should be balanced. Calculator use in the early grades certainly calls for balance.

Consider what is required to use a calculator effectively. First, you must identify the operation you need. Does the problem require multiplication, division, subtraction? Choosing appropriately means that you know enough about how these operations work. Second, you need to be able to judge the reasonableness of the answer to make sure you didn't make a keystroke error.

For example, you are dividing $153.60 by 48 and get $32.00. You immediately recognize the decimal is misplaced. This requires an understanding of place value. Or maybe you get $9.45 for an answer. Because you know multiplication/division facts you estimate quickly that the number should be closer to $3.00, not $9.00. Using a calculator well actually requires substantial facility with mathematical concepts and facts, but without the heavy lifting of paper-and-pencil computation.

By the time our students are in sixth grade, they should not only be using calculators well, they should be using spreadsheet software to conduct data experiments and explore ratio and proportion. They have a lot to do to be ready for algebra in middle school. They don't have the time to waste doing long division with just paper and pencil.

WRITING AND PUBLISHING

From the first moment computers entered classrooms they have been used for writing. Elementary students still report that they use word processing more than any other computer application at school. The beauty of word processing is that it has taken the exhaustive labor out of drafting and revising. Correcting, reorganizing, and rewriting on a computer make the writing process something fluid, not just a series of steps to follow in sequence.

Because the computer makes revising relatively painless, teachers can demand better written products from children. It's easy to send students back several times to make adjustments to a computer draft if it's needed. It's much harder, not to mention traumatic, to ask students for multiple revisions when each new draft requires them to write the whole piece out by hand. Word processing also places the mechanics of writing in their proper place, as the finish on good writing, not its substance. Spell check doesn't replace knowing how to spell, as many of us who use word processors every day know too well. It won't tell you, for example, that you used *there* when you meant *their*. But it is a helpful tool when putting the final spit and polish on a piece.

Today's computers also have the capacity to produce multimedia reports and presentations easily and cheaply. Images can be scanned or downloaded from CD-ROM software or the Internet and imported into print documents. LCD displays allow for slide presentations with sound and animation. This capacity challenges our conventional notions about what it means to "publish."

We are not going to argue that visual and audio displays, no matter how elaborate, substitute for written work, especially for the depth of understanding that written texts develop and demand. But we also recognize that the world bombards students with information in visual and audio form as well as in print. Young people need to develop the skills that will enable them to be critical consumers of the information explosion. They must begin early so they understand how advertisements, for example, are used to manipulate them into wanting certain products. In using different media to communicate their own ideas, students are better able to interpret the information that saturates their airspace day after day. Youngsters who learn to control messages are not likely to be controlled by them.

RESEARCH

The capacity for research is by far the most significant contribution the Internet makes to education. A computer terminal and a phone line are all that's needed to connect to the world. With just a few keystrokes we can be linked to the spectrum of information and ideas about anything and everything, to the work of artists and musicians everywhere, and even to phenomena occurring in real time. The Internet also puts us in touch with the undesirable side of humanity—angry souls, predators, racists. Because the Internet provides an unfiltered platform accessible to all with a computer, its strength for students is also its weakness.

Teaching children to use this wonderful medium while protecting them from its unwelcome elements is tricky business. Software is now available that helps screen out so-called adult content, which alleviates immediate worries about explicit material. But no one yet has developed a search engine that will answer the researcher's fundamental question: Is this source credible?

For example, a quick search on the topic "global warming" produced over one million hits. The top ten included U.S. and Canadian government agencies for environmental protection, environmental advocacy groups, and issue-oriented institutes. Students accessing these sites would find out that there is a problem but the government can manage it; that the problem is huge and the government is not doing enough because they are cowed by the interests of big business; and that the problem is overblown and the government is overreacting to the detriment of individual freedom and free enterprise. All assertions are backed with scientific claims.

When students are in contact with the range of opinion and punditry, the skills they have developed in the subject areas, especially in science and social studies, will equip them to sort the wheat from the chaff. "Who says so?" becomes the first question students will ask when they examine a new source. Are these legitimate scientists, historians, or analysts? Does this organization or agency have a vested interest in promoting a particular point of view? Children will need guidance as they navigate these waters. But by the end of elementary school they should know that some sources are more credible than others and begin to evaluate them on their own, so that they will be suspicious when they pull up a web page claiming that the Holocaust never happened.

Our young students will also be using the Internet to communicate through e-mail, message boards, and chat rooms. Connecting students personally to others outside of their own little worlds builds understanding like no textbook. At the same time, it's important for students to know the protocols of Internet communication, the rules governing plagiarism, and other customs for being on-line. The free-for-all of Net culture requires users to exercise a great sense of responsibility that they should practice from the first time they go on-line.

We don't want to leave the impression that allowing elementary students to use the Internet is like casting them into the vast unknown without a lifeline. There are fabulous opportunities on-line for students to learn much more than can be found in the library stacks. Youngsters can track the progress of hurricanes along with meteorologists, work collaboratively on a science project with students on the other side of the world, and watch pictures of the solar system being transmitted by the *Voyager* spacecraft. And no doubt, this is only the beginning.

PROFESSIONAL DEVELOPMENT FOR TEACHERS

The value of computer technology to teachers also cannot be overstated. The Internet can connect them to their professional organizations and colleagues across the country. They can easily stay up-to-date with research in their fields and discover how different practices are working in real classrooms. The Net is also becoming an ever-expanding reservoir of lesson plans and curriculum.

But while the resources are rich and extensive, there is no quality control. For every challenging and interesting lesson there are a dozen pieces of academic fluff, as we showed in our discussion of multiple intelligences in chapter four. Teachers must know their sources. They must also analyze the lessons against their state or district standards to make sure they are aligned and rigorous.

Net-savvy professional groups and researchers have begun to provide professional development on-line.[11] The best of these provide limited-access areas on the Web where teachers from across the country can exchange student work, assignments, and lesson plans and examine the work for its capacity to help students meet standards. The input of teachers from different places has the effect of ratcheting up content; quality isn't allowed to slip under the collaborative scrutiny of the profession.

TECH-READY CLASSROOMS

Some teachers are milking technology for all its benefits. They are not only using computers for instruction, they use e-mail to stay in contact with parents and colleagues and mine the Internet for ideas and resources. But many more teachers have been slow to make much use of this resource, despite the fact that nearly all of them report having access to a computer either at home or at school. Time—always a scarcity for teachers—is a big problem. Time is required, of course, just to learn how to use the equipment.

Teachers also cite not having enough time for trying out new software. Unlike textbooks, which can be skimmed and reviewed fairly quickly, a software package must be loaded up and explored to evaluate its instructional worth. Another problem teachers report is not having enough machines available for students to complete an assignment within a reasonable amount of time. The encouraging news on that front is that teachers who have more computers in their classrooms tend to use much more digital content.[12]

But if the lack of time is a present problem, the passage of time is bound to bring solutions. Communities continue to invest in classroom computers. Eventually, they will become as standard as a textbook. Distance learning through costly satellite feeds will become more affordable as this technology becomes more prevalent. Young teachers coming out of education school today are already more comfortable about using digital content in their classrooms.

The future challenge for technology is not whether it will be in the classroom, but how well it will be used.

NOTES

1. National Telecommunications and Information Administration, *Falling Through the Net.*

2. U.S. Department of Education, *Internet Access in U.S. Public Schools and Classrooms.* Ninety-five percent of all schools and 94 percent of elementary schools had access in 1999.

3. National Telecommunications and Information Administration, *Falling Through the Net.*

4. U.S. Department of Education, *Internet Access in U.S. Public Schools and Classrooms.*

5. U.S. Department of Education, *Student Computer Use.*

6. Education Week, *Technology Counts 98.*

7. Katz, *Geeks.*

8. Armstrong, "ADD as a Social Invention."

9. Ibid.

10. U.S. Department of Education, *National Assessment of Education Progress (NAEP) 1996 National Mathematics Results.*

11. To our knowledge, there are three flourishing on-line professional development services available to teachers. Significantly, one such service has already come and gone—an indication of the cutthroat competitiveness of the market.

12. Fatemi, "Building the Digital Curriculum."

CHAPTER SEVEN

LET'S SEE
IF THIS
WORKED

ACCOUNTABILITY HANGS over all education—even that of the youngest children—in the first decade of this century. The emphasis on testing is perceived to have originated in the development of standards and within a generally critical attitude toward education. Accountability is also the rallying cry in state houses and in the U.S. Congress: a widespread perception that schools have been doing a poor job led everywhere to calls for tests to lay bare the awful truth. To many people, it seems as if testing rather than learning is the aim. Although accountability means in essence reporting to the taxpayers about how public money has been spent, it seems to many people, often the best intentioned, as cruel and unusual punishment. That is because in classrooms and schools, accountability means tests, and tests are perceived as an unnecessary imposition on schools by hostile and unfeeling legislators.

However, testing has been a feature of the educational landscape for most of the last century. What is new and different is the use of tests: their results now have consequences, and the data they supply can be used to judge not only students, but also teachers, schools, and districts.

When benchmarks at grade levels, especially 4 and 8, were enforced with tests, the effects of tests became serious as never before. Students in

Chicago, New York, Washington, D.C., Los Angeles, and Long Beach, California, just to name a few large city systems, cannot proceed to the next higher grade if their test scores are not satisfactory. In Texas students cannot graduate if they have not passed the Grade 10 Texas Assessment of Academic Skills (TAAS). Now in more and more states, schools are subject to sanction if their students do not perform at satisfactory levels on tests. Sanctions include the complete restaffing of failing schools, and even the closing of schools and redistribution of students to other schools.

These apparently harsh accountability measures have drawn opposition from groups such as FairTest, the Mexican-American Legal Defense Fund, and other civil rights organizations. Their argument rests on the denial of expected benefits (especially a graduation diploma) resulting from failure on a single test, because there may be racial bias in tests that produce such large numbers of failing students among minority groups.

Opposition of this kind to testing and accountability conceals an assumption—that tests are essentially punitive, unfair by their very nature. While this assumption may rest on painful personal experiences, transferred into concern for social justice, it is at bottom a misunderstanding of what testing is for and why it is part of all education from prekindergarten on up.

THE FUNCTION OF TESTING

Testing produces information, nothing more and nothing less, about what has been learned. The result of testing is feedback—information essential to students, teachers, parents, administrators, and policy makers. Learning anything is impossible without a feedback mechanism to tell what has been learned and what needs reinforcing—or even teaching again from the beginning. A little thought about any form of learning will demonstrate the essential role of assessment: a child learning to talk finds out what brings results and corrects when tests—intended communication with others—don't produce the right toy or tidbit; learning to play a musical instrument is a constant try-test-feedback system; a new program on a computer requires learning, and then the learner says, "Let's see if this worked."

That phrase is the key to understanding testing. Any test or assessment is asking the question, "Did it work?" so that teachers and learners find out what worked and what didn't, and what they need to go back and work on. Standards clearly need to be supported by tests—how can we know whether students have learned if we don't test them?

Another major misunderstanding often stands in the way of clear judgment about tests: tests are dipsticks into children's knowledge and skills, they don't report on everything that they know. The standards are now the domain of expected knowledge and skills, but no test can report on the learning of all of them. A test by its nature samples learning.

FORMATIVE AND SUMMATIVE ASSESSMENT

A preliminary definition: *testing* and *assessment* are essentially the same thing—the words can be treated as synonyms. Sometimes the phrase "assessment tests" is seen in the press—it's a tautology.

The testing or assessment that goes on in the classroom daily is *formative* assessment. Any activity that gives information about what has been learned can be seen as formative assessment: when the children in the Houston classrooms we described in the last chapter were chanting their alphabets or their numbers by fives and tens, that was formative assessment. So too are the tests given every five lessons to see where students are in reading, writing, and computation so that they can be moved into different groups according to their progress. Portfolios kept for each student are formative assessment; to some extent, so is homework and even daily assignments.

Everyone likes formative assessment. When we talk about standards and assessments, one of the first questions from the audience is usually about standardized tests: "Why do we have to have them?" "Couldn't we just have portfolios scored by classroom teachers?" These questions, it seems, are motivated by two underlying assumptions: testing is all right when performed by people who know the students, so that they can make allowances for different circumstances; and testing should include more than a sample of students' work—it should show everything that they know and can do.

The other kind of testing, *summative,* draws fire because its characteristics are exactly the reverse of these assumptions: it is designed by people who do not know the student and can make no allowances, and it samples their work. Summative assessment sums up and reports on students' learning, often to a higher authority such as the district, the state, or the nation.

For the students' sake, summative assessment is as necessary as formative assessment. Precisely because teachers and parents know students well, their judgment of their academic achievements can be colored by that knowledge. They may be motivated by their affectionate knowledge of the children to inflate their achievements in ways that will damage them. A 1994 study by the U.S. Department of Education collected data that showed a distressing situation: students in high-poverty schools receive As and Bs for work that receives Cs and Ds in suburban schools. We would not know about this if it were not for summative tests. The students' grades were compared to their scores on a national test: the students who got As and Bs in the poor and minority schools scored *below* the 50th percentile, approximately the same achievement level as C and D students in the suburban schools.

So summative tests are necessary to give students and schools an accurate picture of their achievement, precisely because they are designed by people who don't know the students.

STANDARDIZED TESTS

What seems to upset people is the formalization characteristic of summative assessment. Tests are events specially calendared, set apart from the normal routine. If we understand formalization as a necessary evil, not a threat or a punishment, its fangs can be drawn and the tension reduced.

The most obvious characteristic of this formalization is the fact that these tests are standardized. Despite all the assumptions about standardization, it means nothing more than that tests are given in uniform conditions—they are given at the same time to all the students, using the same no. 2 pencils, answering the same questions, with the same directions, and with the same amount of time to complete the test. That's all standardized means.

It doesn't mean that the test is multiple-choice or that it is norm-referenced. In fact, if portfolios are used for large-scale testing, they have to be standardized. Standardization has nothing to do with standards—it refers to another meaning of the word *standard,* the meaning in the phrase "standard issue."

Standardization ensures that the test is measuring what the students put on the paper in a certain amount of time, and that the results can be compared to what they were expected to learn. It should prevent one kind of cheating because all students are taking the test at the same time and can't tell each other the questions.

But the formalization necessary to ensure standardization is threatening, especially to elementary schools, teachers, and the children. They have to be prepared for the test, and some, especially the younger ones, may have the same reactions as when they are facing a visit to the doctor—they may be told over and over that it's good for them but they absolutely refuse to believe it. On the whole, young children reflect the attitudes of adults around them, and if the adults make no fuss, the children won't either.

However, young children seem to be much more robust in their ability to withstand the rigors of testing than previously thought. Ten years ago it was accepted doctrine among educators of young children that standardized tests were too stressful for the children and for that reason could not yield accurate information about their academic achievement. But it became clear that the information tests yield is so valuable in allowing early diagnosis of reading and other cognitive difficulties that mild discomfort is justified in order to be able to help the child succeed.

THE EFFECTS OF TESTING ON TEACHING

Like most things in life, the effects of testing on teaching can be both good and bad. A lot of people know only about the presumably adverse effects—and we'll deal with those in the next section in this chapter on teaching to the test.

That there are beneficial effects of testing on classroom instruction may seem less surprising when we examine the relationship among standards, instruction, and testing. Teaching necessarily has a goal—children's learning. In having a goal, teaching is like most of our activities, for as humans we are essentially goal-oriented.

Now, however, that goal, instead of being somewhat nebulous—learning in general—is clearly specified in the standards. As we have shown in chapter three, students must be able to read skillfully by the end of grade 3 and must have learned enough mathematics to be able to tackle algebra by the end of grade 6, to give just two examples.

Because of this three-way relationship (standards, tests, instruction), children in many inner-city and rural schools are learning to read and learning more mathematics than they would if there were no tests. In Texas, TAAS is aimed at ensuring that children in border schools who speak no English when they enter school are taught as much as children in the wealthy suburbs of Dallas. In Kent County, Maryland, an Eastern Shore community with small rural schools and stagnant poverty, the students beat all the odds on the Maryland School Performance Assessment Program (MSPAP). The Kent County third-graders outscored all other districts in Maryland: 75.6 percent scored at proficient or above. The superintendent, the principals, and the teachers analyzed what it required and made sure that they were teaching the knowledge and skills.[1]

Instead of asking about tests, "Are they testing what we teach?" teachers must ask, "Are we teaching what they test?"

We're talking about the summative tests here, of course, the standardized tests designed by state authorities or national test makers. If teachers align their formative tests to the standards, then everything will be pointing in the same direction.

TEACHING TO THE TEST

In an atmosphere of intense focus on accountability, charges that the curriculum is being narrowed to the contents of the test are heard frequently.[2] To get at the real issues involved in "teaching to the test," we must consider three possible meanings of the phrase: teaching to the test, teaching the test (and nothing more), and cheating.

It's easiest to start with the last one. Earlier this year a principal of an elementary school in one of the wealthiest counties in the United States, Montgomery County in Maryland (actually a suburb of Washington, D.C.), was forced to resign because she and her teachers had watched children as they took the test and suggested different answers to them. That's cheating. Testing companies are wary of erasures on answer sheets and will conduct investigations if they find a series of them, for some teachers have been known to erase answers and substitute correct ones. That's cheating.

Teaching the test means narrowing what is taught until it matches just the test content and nothing more. It's pretty hard to do unless many practice copies of the test are available. Teaching the test is an attempt to short-circuit the connection between the standards and the test: instead of teaching what students are expected to know and be able to do, teachers try to figure out what's on the test and teach only that. They also mimic the form of the test by asking for multiple-choice answers on assignments. Teaching the test is also cheating, for it cheats the students out of the knowledge and skills that are not tested, probably the majority of the material they need.

However, teaching to the test as we have defined it is neither of these: it means knowing how the test relates to the standards and teaching those concepts and applications that will prepare students to succeed on the test. Judith Langer of the National Research Center on English Learning and Achievement did research on teaching to the test in middle and high schools, but the lessons of her research apply equally well to elementary schools. In schools that performed well on the test, Langer writes,

> Teachers, principals, and district-level coordinators even take the test themselves to identify the skills and knowledge required to do well. They discuss how these demands relate to district and state standards and expectations as well as to their curriculum, and then they discuss ways to integrate these skills into the curriculum.... This process helps them move the focus of test preparation from practice on the surface features of the test itself to the knowledge that underlies successful learning and achievement in literacy and English.[3]

This supports the message we want to send as clearly as we can: Teach the standards and the test will take care of itself. Teaching to the standards is teaching to the test.

Doing so will also take care of some of the anxiety that will invade schools when the test is changed. If tests are based on standards, and children have learned to the standards, then in theory there should be little threat in different tests.

But of course students do have to know what they are facing, and practicing on the form of the tests is only humane. Students have to know how to fill in the bubbles attached to multiple-choice tests. Even more important in many schools is learning how to write answers to open-ended questions. In Maryland a few years of experience were necessary to get students and teachers used to the form of MSPAP. They had been used to multiple-choice and had to switch to open-ended responses that often stretched over several days. It took a while for everyone to realize that MSPAP tests are also good instructional units, so that in this case teaching to the test is also good teaching.[4]

WHO DESIGNS TESTS AND WHAT THEY LOOK LIKE

As we said in the introduction, almost all states are either using or contemplating a state test to measure school and student performance. These tests tend to fall into two groups: tests designed by the teachers of the state (like the MSPAP) and refined psychometrically by experts, and tests purchased from test publishers.

Those purchased from test publishers are usually based on the national standards, not those of the state—although as we have frequently pointed out, there isn't a great deal of difference in most cases. These tests have names like the TerraNova (published by CTB/McGraw-Hill); Stanford 9 (published by Harcourt Educational Measurement, the Psychological Corporation); and the Iowa Test of Basic Skills (ITBS) (published by the Riverside Publishing Company). Many other companies are engaged in the development and scoring of tests, although their names are less well known; for example, Data Recognition, Measurement Incorporated, Measured Progress, and National Computer Systems.

Tests used by states (such as TAAS or the Ohio Proficiency Tests [OPT]) consist of items and questions developed or selected by the state's teachers and then refined technically by national test developers. Such state tests bear the name of the state, unlike the Stanford 9 or the TerraNova. For example, TAAS is designed by Harcourt Educational Measurement but does not bear the company's name. These are all summative tests, although practice and sample tests can (and should) be used in the classroom formatively.

The bulk of the questions in the published tests are multiple-choice. They look like this example from a third-grade mathematics test:

Four friends went to buy doughnuts. Anne bought 4, Joan bought 6, Juan bought 5, and Tamika bought 7. What would you do to find out how many doughnuts they bought all together?

(a) Add
(b) Subtract
(c) Multiply
(d) Divide

Some published tests do have open-ended questions, often called performance assessments, but these are more often found in tests constructed for states. They look like this, an example of an eighth-grade mathematics performance assessment:

A pattern of dots is shown below. At each step, more dots are added to the pattern. The number of dots added at each step is more than the number added in the previous step. The pattern continues infinitely.

Marcy has to determine the number of dots in the 20th step, but she does not want to draw all 20 pictures and then count the dots. Explain and show how she could do this and give the answer Marcy should get for the number of dots.

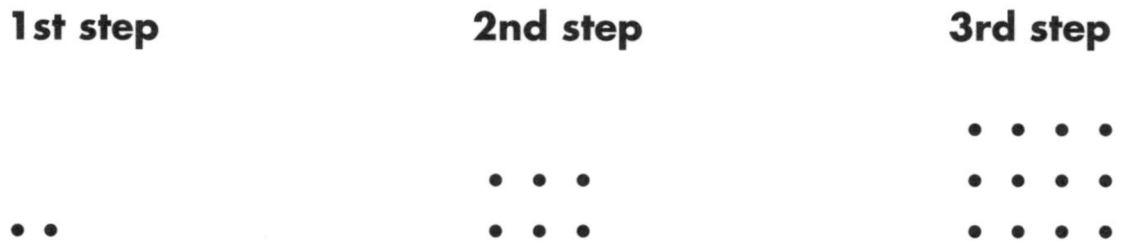

1st step   **2nd step**   **3rd step**

Source: NAEP 1996, Grade 8

The important diference between multiple-choice and performance assessments is that multiple-choice asks the students to *select* a correct answer, and performance assessments ask the students to *provide* the answer themselves. This means that it is possible to get a multiple-choice question right by guessing, or even by chance, but it isn't possible to do that with constructed-response or open-ended questions (unless the child copies from the student in the next seat).

All test publishers can supply both multiple-choice and performance assessments, but there's a trade-off in deciding which to use. Multiple-choice questions can be machine-scored and are therefore cheaper to score. Performance assessments must be scored by groups who must be trained carefully so that all agree on the qualities of work required for certain scores. On the other hand, multiple-choice tends to promote passive learning as it requires only recognition of answers, while performance assessments promote active learning and foster the teaching of writing in all subject areas.

The choice depends on what the authority buying the test (the state education agency or the local education agency—the district) is willing to spend on assessment. On the whole, education agencies become tight-fisted when they start to think about assessment, despite their obsession with accountability. They would be well advised to think about the relationship among the standards, test, and instruction and what qualities in a test promote student achievement of standards.

NORM-REFERENCED AND STANDARDS-BASED TESTS

If a test report comes home and the results are reported in percentiles, the chances are that the students were tested with a norm-referenced test. If the report instead says that the student is at the Basic, Apprentice, Proficient, or Advanced level, then the students took a standards-based or criterion-referenced test. To be sure, parents should ask their school principals: "Was this a norm-referenced or standards-based test?"

Norm-referenced test results are reported according to a normal distribution or bell curve. The tests are designed so that they will distribute half of the students above the middle point and half below the middle point of the curve. Students at the 80th percentile are on the right side of the bell curve and have performed better than 79 percent of the other students who took the test.

Norm-referenced tests provide no information about what students know in terms of what they should know—only how well they did in relation to other students. Students could be at the 80th percentile, but the pool of students—the norm—could have performed so poorly that they lack some essential skill, such as reading comprehension. The problem is compounded by the fact that test publishers sell different norms to school districts: there are national norms, Catholic-school norms, suburban norms, inner-city norms. Students who do well on the inner-city norm would be unlikely to do well judged on the suburban norm.

These facts about norm-referenced tests are largely unknown to parents, even to teachers, for the tests are examined and selected far from the classroom, in central offices in districts and in state education offices in states.

On the other hand, standards-based tests (which used to be called criterion-referenced tests) are tests whose results are reported using levels of achievement. Early results on new standards-based tests have frequently been depressing because few students achieved at the Advanced, even the Proficient levels, and the gap between white, middle-class students and poor, minority, and inner-city students is glaring.

But in a standards-based system, that's what we want to know—where are our students in relation to the standards? We don't need to know whether Maria is better than Juan at multiplication with two digits, or whether their school is better or worse than West Street Elementary School next door. We want to know where each of them and their school are on the way to achieving the grade 3, 4, 5, or 6 standards.

A norm-referenced test is used for the purpose of sorting out students by comparing them to each other. When a preliminary test is designed, it is tried out on students, usually in schools near to the cities where test publishers are located. If most students do well on some items, those items will be removed from the pool. If they remained, students would probably get them all right and thus would not be spread out on the bell curve. So in order to ensure sorting, items that are a little trickier, not what everyone could get, are substituted.

This means that the test is not likely to ask only about knowledge central to the subject, but also to ask about peripheral bits of information that not all students might know. It is possible for students to know the essentials of a subject well but not be able to answer less familiar questions presented in a way intended to catch the unwary.

Standards-based tests are designed differently. Test designers distill the essence of what students should know and be able to do from the standards, and then design questions and test items directly connected to them. Each item or question is scored as evidence of reaching, partially reaching, or not reaching the standard. Theoretically, in a standards-based test, it is possible for all the students to score at the Advanced level—and it would be a tribute to their teachers and their own learning if they did so.

The results of norm-referenced tests and standards-based tests cannot be compared, no matter what statistical magic is attempted. Those who claim to do so are deceiving the public with psychometric smoke and mirrors. Norm-referenced tests and standards-based tests are designed to do different jobs, themselves incompatible.[5] In fact, comparison of tests across states has been found to be impossible, adding to the difficulty of obtaining reliable information about student achievement throughout the United States.[6]

TOWARD BETTER TESTING

We would be the last to argue that testing as it is today is uniformly beneficial to students. We know it isn't. In many cases it is a necessary evil—but nevertheless necessary. Without the information that test results provide, we would not know on the classroom level which children need specific kinds of help, and on the state and national levels, where to invest resources for increased knowledge.

Testing can and should be better than it is. Tests should be aligned with standards in every case so that we are not confused by comparisons with other students as well as comparisons with standards. Tests should include a larger proportion of performance assessments, which can become models for curriculum, as in the case of MSPAP. Where there are high stakes on summative assessments—as in the case of promotion/retention decisions at grade 4 or grade 6—information from formative assessments, such as portfolios, should be included.

Alignment is the key—with the standards, with classroom assessments, with grades. Many school districts are now revising report cards to align with standards so that grades will not be as widely divergent from test scores as they may have been. All the information we have about student performance should tell us—and the students—the truth consistently about where they stand in progress toward the standards.

NOTES

1. "Writing Skills Key to Success on MD Tests," B1.

2. Foremost among critics who charge that the curriculum is confined to test contents is Professor Linda McNeil of Rice University in Houston, who claims that "TAAS drills are becoming the curriculum in our poorest schools" (testimony in federal court case brought by the Mexican-American Legal Defense and Education Fund against the Texas Assessment of Academic Skills).

3. Langer, *Guidelines for Teaching Middle and High School Students to Read and Write Well.*

4. The MSPAP assessments are designed by groups of teachers in Maryland who develop them during the summer and then use them during the school year. Some of the ideas are refined into tests by psychometricians, but large numbers of units are available for anyone's use. Because MSPAP tests at grades 3, 5, and 8, the publicly available units are especially useful for elementary schools. Maryland Assessment Consortium, http://mac.cl.k12.md.us.2000/general info/facts.html.

5. Test publishers all claim that they can offer reporting by norm and by level, but the major national tests—Stanford 9, TerraNova, ITBS—are all designed as norm-referenced tests. Thus when standards-based reporting by level is offered, its value is questionable, because the test is designed as a norm-referenced test and not redesigned for standards-based reporting.

6. The only nationally administered test is the National Assessment of Educational Progress (NAEP), which has no individual student results. The NAEP offers states the opportunity to participate for comparison purposes, but not all states take the opportunity.

CHAPTER EIGHT

RECOMMENDATIONS: HOW ALL ELEMENTARY STUDENTS CAN REACH THE STANDARDS

THROUGHOUT THIS BOOK we have emphasized the change that has taken place in the model of education in the United States during the last ten years. We were groping toward it in the first edition of *Smart Start,* but now the model has come into focus through the development of standards, and in many cases, aligned assessments.

Elementary education is now focused on ends, not means: all children will read at grade 1 and be able to use reading to learn by grade 3; all children will be ready for algebra by the end of grade 6. But how they are taught and how they learn is a matter for the collective judgment of the school community—teachers, administrators, parents, and school-board members.

We have talked a good deal about teachers throughout the earlier chapters, so in this chapter we will turn to the responsibility of those outside the classroom for understanding and supporting standards-based education.

POLICIES THAT HELP

The success of standards-based reform will ultimately be decided in classrooms. But state and district policy makers also make decisions that will either support schools' efforts to improve or squash them before they have a chance to have an effect. In this book we profiled schools where all students consistently meet high standards. The happy news is that they were easier to find at the end of the decade than they were when we wrote the first edition in 1991. Yet they are still exceptions to the rule. These schools succeed because of the inspiration of the principal, the willingness of the faculty to change, and all too often because of the many long hours the staff puts in above and beyond what we can reasonably demand. As a country, we can't afford to allow excellence to be random and heroic. Every child deserves a good education. The system must provide it.

Policy makers have taken the first major step by establishing high standards for student learning. Many states have followed up with assessments and accountability for results in order to assure the public that the new standards are being met. The first among these are beginning to see schools work for all children, particularly at the elementary level. In a few states, whole districts are meeting high standards.

But the work of policy makers is far from over. Governors, legislators, state education trustees, and local school-board members need to craft policies that are helpful to schools, even while they insist on results. They also need to back up their standards with targeted resources so that systems can meet new goals. Voters and advocates need to support policies that will benefit all students and send a message to elected officials that good schools are a very high priority.

NO PAIN, NO GAIN?

After some controversy in the mid-1990s, almost everyone now agrees that standards are a good thing. In fact, when we talk to people across the country, they are often surprised to find out that there haven't always been standards for U.S. education. There is also support for testing students and using the results to judge the effectiveness of schools with consequences for continued poor performance. But what people support in the abstract can begin to break down in the details. Accountability appears to be a sensible policy until it's your school and your child. That's when people start to get nervous.

Several accountability systems have been put in place without inducing widespread panic, while others have been seriously threatened by teacher and parent backlash. It's to be expected that schools wouldn't exactly welcome accountability. They have been able to operate for a long time without having to show evidence that children are learning. Now continued low student achievement can result in sanctions against schools, including the possibility of a state takeover.

For the most part, though, schools have complied with new policies even if it hasn't always been a happy transition. This is especially true in places where the new standards came with extra resources for implementation and a reasonable timetable that allowed schools to adjust to new demands. A few commendable states have designed their accountability systems so that low-performing schools receive additional funds and technical support to further assist their transition. After all, the goal is not to punish schools, but to make them work for all children. And as schools begin to see results, principals and teachers often rally behind the new accountability systems themselves.

Other states, however, have met with resistance not just from schools, but from parents. One of the most difficult issues in school accountability is determining how much of the burden the individual student should bear. Students' motivation to do well can be a key factor in their learning. It hardly seems right to judge adults for student achievement if students aren't putting forth their best effort. On the other hand, students are unlikely to be motivated by mind-numbing instruction, especially when delivered incompetently or indifferently.

While there is a general sense that both schools and students have responsibility for learning, state policy is mixed. Some states are only concerned with school performance. There are no consequences for individual students based on their scores on the state assessment. But a growing number of states have policies with repercussions for both schools and students whose performance on state assessments is now linked to promotion policies, including high school graduation. It's in the latter states that parents are expressing the most concern.

Elementary schoolchildren are generally spared the full force of accountability. Unlike their older siblings in high school, young children are still motivated to please adults and will do their best on tests regardless of their purpose. But they are not completely immune from personal consequences. Some states and districts are implementing promotion policies that affect early elementary students who have not yet mastered reading or math. To some adults, the policies seem draconian: children who don't hit the passing score do not proceed to the next grade level. Summer school is typically required for these students to give them a chance to catch up. But if by the end of the summer they still don't pass the test it's back to the grade they just finished.

Chicago was one of the first districts to establish such a policy. So far the results could be viewed as a glass half full or half empty: as many as two-thirds of the children referred to summer school are being promoted to the next grade alongside their peers; but the children who don't pass return to their previous grade level. To date, the children who are retained in grade aren't showing much academic improvement.

Reform happens one classroom at a time. Stories about failures give the reform critics ammunition to topple standards before they have a real chance. We prefer to dwell on the success stories: the schools, principals, and teachers—like those we profiled in this book—who expect all students to meet standards and make sure that they do. We also support policies that no longer permit children to pass through elementary grades without learning to read with comprehension or be mathematically competent. Accountability only seems harsh until one considers the alternative—more and more children left behind.

However, there are ways to implement standards-based reform that work better than others. Policy makers, educators, and the public need to pay careful attention so that standards can be made to work well. In this chapter we discuss several of these issues.

Assessments

Nearly every state assesses students at regular intervals as a measure of school effectiveness. Yet many of the tests currently used for this purpose are not aligned to the state standards. Instead, several states administer off-the-shelf norm-referenced tests and hold schools accountable for the scores. As we showed in chapter seven, such tests are designed only to tell us that some students perform better than others, not whether students have the knowledge and skills embedded in the standards. Relying on norm-referenced tests for accountability, therefore, is illogical; someone has to be below average, even if every test-taker does well.

Because standards- or criterion-based assessments provide information about progress on standards, they should be the only tests used for accountability and decision making about schools and students. It is also essential for these assessments to be aligned to the state or district standards. Tests that aren't aligned send conflicting messages to schools and teachers about what they should be teaching. The mismatch could also result from the kind of test used. For example, standards that ask students to explain, analyze, or persuade are not going to be served well by a multiple-choice-only format, especially one dominated by questions that ask for simple recognition of information or the single application of a procedure.

States and districts need to make sure that the tests they use for accountability tell them whether students are meeting their standards. Commercial tests may serve this purpose. Several states have opted to develop their own. Either way, how well the test aligns with standards must be the deciding factor, not cost. In addition, states have a responsibility to get the results back to schools quickly and in a form useful for teachers and parents to make informed decisions about instruction. Giving schools a single numerical score on a math test, for example, tells them little about how well they performed in computation versus problem solving.

Neither does it help to bombard principals and teachers with pages of raw data. State departments of education and central offices should provide data electronically and in formats that are easy to understand, analyze, and communicate to teachers and parents.

Curriculum

Just like assessments, curriculum needs to be aligned to standards. We have made the point throughout this book that standards can open up a wealth of curricular choices for schools and teachers because many roads will lead to the same destination. This is not to say that any road will get there. Present curriculums must be analyzed for their ability to move students toward the high levels of knowledge and skill demanded by standards. In many if not most cases, the curriculum will have to be replaced.

Writing curriculum, planning units, designing tasks and assignments, choosing texts, developing scoring guides—all this takes time. And time for teachers is already in short supply. State departments of education or district central offices often provide some assistance by writing curriculum guides and adopting textbooks. But these are limited in helping teachers cope day-to-day with implementing new content. Some states attempt to fill in the gaps by maintaining an on-line bank of "standards-based" lesson plans. But usually the quality of the items is not rigorously controlled. A lot of it is the same old stuff dressed up with new objectives. Too much of it falls into that large category of "fun things for kids to do" that lack an explicit academic focus.

Policy makers need to allocate more resources for the development of curriculum, lesson plans, and scoring guides aligned to standards, and for the systematic review of textbooks, software, and other classroom resources. These materials must pass demanding criteria that administrators, teachers, and the public can trust. While we are not arguing for states to mandate a specific curriculum, we are saying that teachers need a reliable supply of resources they can choose from to use in their classrooms. They don't have time to do it all on their own.

Professional Development

The most urgent need for resources is for professional development of teachers. Instituting a system that promises all students will meet high standards is nothing short of an educational revolution. The present cadre of teachers was not prepared to deliver this level of content to this many children. It's not only unfair, it's counterproductive to make a profession accountable without also giving them the tools they need to accomplish the task. Foremost on this list is giving them strategies, content, and above all *time* for retooling.

Here is how Dennis Sparks, executive director of the National Staff Development Council, describes the kind of professional development needed:

> The rationale for the importance of teacher development is not exactly rocket science: to be successful in teaching all students to high standards, teachers need to be engaged in sustained, intellectually rigorous study of what they teach and how they teach it. Teachers learn better when they learn together and support one another in planning better lessons, improving the quality of their students' work, and in solving the day-to-day problems of teaching and learning.[1]

Teachers, like all professionals, need to stay current with new research and developments in their field. For this reason, most districts already devote considerable dollars to staff development. But it's usually training on the fly. Teachers typically get a mixed bag of isolated workshops covering a scattered array of fashionable education topics. Few of these workshops concern academic content. In general, they also lack any comprehensive plans for follow-up support, and the lessons are lost when teachers return to their classrooms and fall back on old habits. Teachers receive rewards for their own individual efforts at continuing professional growth—mostly in pedagogical theory, rarely for scholarship. They gain certificates that are not instructionally centered, for example in counseling or administration.

Effective professional development must be ongoing and on-site. The Brooklyn elementary school we visited is a model. The school maintains full-time "staff developers," exemplary teachers whose only job is to work with new teachers and to plan and facilitate continuous training in the school. All teachers convene for bimonthly meetings with their grade-level colleagues to plan curriculum, design lessons, and examine student work. These meetings, facilitated by the staff developer, are devoted exclusively to exploring instruction that will produce student gains. The meetings are also noteworthy for being an integral part of the regular school day. Teachers are not brought in after school or on Saturdays for staff development. Neither are they released for the occasional staff development day to attend a potpourri of workshops and training sessions. The Brooklyn school has found the resources to build this time into professional schedules. In addition to paying for the staff developers, the school has enough reading specialists and art, music, and P.E. teachers to free up classroom teachers during the day. They also are able to make good use of parent volunteers.

Another key ingredient in effective professional development is a focus on standards. The Brooklyn school used its scheduled time well. Standards informed the agenda of every team meeting. Instruction and subject matter were inseparable parts of the work. Finally, the team approach ensures that teachers have the support of peers while they try to implement new lessons or methods. They are not left to flail about on their own, only to find it's easier to return to familiar ground.

There are other districts across the country that build planning time into the regular schedule for elementary teachers, often by sending the children home for a half day every week. However, there is usually no set structure for this time. Teachers who have this benefit often use it to grade papers and plan their own classroom schedules. A staff developer in the building who could organize this time better is almost unheard of.

More room is needed in education budgets for professional development: first by staffing individuals on-site whose sole responsibility is planning and facilitating continuous training, and second by helping schools find time in the weekly schedule for team meetings, either by sending children home or by adding more resource teachers. District offices especially need to maintain some quality control over professional development activities to make sure their investment is paying off in higher student achievement; for example, by requiring that the professional development activities connected to school reform programs show proof that they raise student achievement.

Technology

It's probably redundant to advise policy makers to invest in technology for schools. States, districts, and corporate givers are already doing this. As we mentioned earlier, even though we don't yet have enough computers in every school to give all students equal access, we are rapidly making gains and will likely close these gaps in a few short years.

But we also stressed that just having the equipment is an insufficient response. There's still a practical problem: many schools lack the technical support to maintain the computers. It should go without saying, but along with the equipment should come the staff to keep it running.

There is an educational issue as well: having technology does not guarantee that it is being used well or that it is increasing student learning. Technology needs to undergo the same quality control as curriculum and professional development. Too often, evaluations of technology in schools are concerned with whether or not students know how to use computers. The real question should be whether students are using computers to become more knowledgeable. If the technology isn't contributing to results, perhaps the investment should be retargeted.

Support for Students

The standards aren't going to budge. All children will need to meet them. However, this does not mean that all students will meet standards at the same time with the same methods. Many students will need extra support to meet standards without falling behind their age group. Schools are beginning to provide extra tutoring, Saturday sessions, summer school, and other supports for struggling students. Some of these strategies are funded through the schools. Others are privately offered by community-based organizations and churches.

Because so many parents work outside the home, before- and after-school care of children has become a major feature of many schools. The school building open from 7:00 A.M. to 9:00 P.M. is not a rarity, and at least one school district is planning to build a school that will be part of a community center, with the public library, a senior center, the community health center, and the recreation center all as part of the same complex. Districts can coordinate the activities in these centers, seizing opportunities to connect services to academic standards to further reinforce student learning.

THE ROLE OF UNIVERSITIES

Universities prepare teachers. Any policy discussion about improving elementary schools must address the training that prospective teachers receive before they enter the classroom. Standards have changed the whole landscape. Elementary teachers not only need a firm academic grounding in standards content, they need a toolbox full of instructional strategies to enable all children to meet standards.

Standards have also brought talk about accountability to the university level. Title II of the federal Higher Education Act now requires colleges and universities that prepare teachers to publicly report the percentage of teacher candidates from their institution who pass the state licensing examination. The idea is to highlight the effectiveness of teacher education programs. There is also a nascent movement in states to establish accountability mechanisms for teacher education that parallel the targets for elementary and secondary schools. In Texas, for example, universities now have to show that at least 70 percent of their education graduates pass the state licensing test in order to maintain their authority to prepare teachers.

An important element of these new requirements is that they should affect the entire university, not just the school of education. The change is significant. It recognizes the vital role that the colleges of arts and sciences also play in developing new teachers. For too long this role has languished, especially for future elementary teachers, whose only postsecondary exposure to subject matter is most likely the general education courses required of all students on campus. No thought has been given in these courses to connecting the curriculum to the content elementary teachers will be expected to teach. If they learn something relevant to their future occupation, it is by accident, not design.

The new standards being implemented across the country for elementary school are considerably higher than in the past. Mathematics and science standards are particularly more robust. Asking that all sixth-graders be ready for algebra, for example, means that teachers need to begin to lay the groundwork in kindergarten. Yet math and science are subjects that elementary teachers have traditionally felt the least comfortable in teaching, even at a time when standards for students were lower. The preparation of elementary teachers needs to be completely restructured.

Universities should begin by forging collaborations between the arts and sciences and the schools of education for the purpose of designing courses for prospective teachers. These collaborations must ensure not only that the content of these courses is connected to elementary standards, but also that the content goes beyond the standards so that elementary teachers can clearly see where the content they teach fits into the academic continuum. These collaborations must also address pedagogy specifically linked to the subject matter.

We can't raise the ante on children's education without also making sure they have teachers who are qualified to teach them to high levels of knowledge and skill.

THE ROLE OF ADMINISTRATORS

The principal sets the tone in the elementary school. Whether the school focuses on student learning or allows administrative nitpicking to dominate school activity depends on the vision of the individual at the helm. Many talented teachers have had their innovative practices squashed by bureaucratically minded administrators. On the other hand, inspirational principals have moved whole schools of average teachers to the highest level of performance.

What the principal does for the school, the superintendent does for the district. The Pennsylvania community we visited has a relatively new superintendent who declares often and publicly that together they will bring all students up to standards. Her enthusiasm has infected all the schools we visited. Principals, teachers, and students themselves all exuded a can-do spirit directed toward accomplishing specific academic goals.

Much has been written about the importance of school leadership to achieving high standards. Unfortunately, while there's a strong consensus that leadership is a vital ingredient, there's little known about exactly which attributes make an effective leader and even less about how to develop them. We do know that focus is essential. This is easier said than done. The distractions to administrators are never-ending. They have to worry about building management, discipline and safety, buses, food service, schedules, computers that don't work, a chronic shortage of substitutes, and deal with a steady stream of upset parents and harassed school-board members. It can seem that academic learning is the smallest serving on their very full plate.

But administrators need to assert themselves as instructional leaders. They must be the ones to maintain the focus on the fundamental academic mission of schools and create a climate of shared purpose. This won't make the administrative details go away. Buses still need to run on time. But it will clearly establish the school's priorities. Principals need to stress standards in all school activities. Staff meetings should always have time for standards-related discussion on the agenda. Principals should also be a familiar presence in classrooms and in teacher team meetings for professional development.

We are used to seeing principals being constantly interrupted as they escort us through their schools by staff needing some administrative this or that. We tagged along with one principal whose attention was equally in demand. However, this time the interruptions were from the children, all of them wanting to know something about their schoolwork. What a difference!

Communities can make it much easier for principals to be instructional leaders in their buildings, of course. Schools should be evaluated on their academic performance, not how well they comply with administrative mandates. This means granting principals considerable latitude in determining how to help children meet standards, including decisions about hiring and the allocation of school funds. A high-performing school shouldn't have to jump through regulatory hoops to conduct business. In addition, a more supportive central office is almost always appreciated and is more likely to foster two-way collaboration between schools and district officials.

THE ROLE OF PARENTS

School isn't the same place it was when we attended. School is different from what it was even ten years ago, as we have repeatedly said throughout this book. The first responsibility of parents is to shed their preconceptions about school based on their own experiences. They should visit classrooms and ask questions in order to find out what is going on, and not jump to premature judgments.

Their second responsibility is to obtain copies of the standards that the school is using and read them. The school may be using state standards, county standards, or even district standards. In any case, copies should be available to parents through the principal's office. Some places require that the standards be given to parents when they enroll their child. Other districts, such as New York City and Pittsburgh, have produced versions of the standards that make them easier to read than the sometimes stiff and awkward phrasing of standards documents.

Just reading standards isn't easy or even helpful to understanding them. The way to get into the standards is to use them, as teachers have begun to discover. For parents, the most obvious way to use standards is to look at their child's homework assignments side-by-side with the standards.

Parents should always check what students are asked to do at home, of course. But now they should check to see whether the assignment is likely to get students to standards. In chapter four we described a study in California that found that after grade 2 students were being asked to do work that was below the standards for that grade level; by grade 5 nearly all the work was as much as two grades below the appropriate standards. If parents had been monitoring homework against standards, they would have noticed the downward spiral and helped to alert teachers to the problem by asking questions.

We are not suggesting that parents should correct teachers or second-guess them. Instead, what needs to be developed is a partnership in which both parents and teachers cooperate to ensure that children are learning what they need. In the case of Andrew, who was slow in learning to read, neither his mother nor his teacher had the tools to measure the dimensions of the problem. Now we have those tools, and they should help to forge a close partnership to prevent other children from suffering Andrew's fate.

Parents should be welcome in elementary schools for the assistance they can give teachers. In classrooms, parents—and grandparents—can hear children read, or they can ask questions about what children have written. Baking cupcakes for birthday parties is no longer the only expectation that schools should have for parent involvement.

Naturally, the major contribution parents make to their children's elementary education is at home, and not only through checking their homework. Parents of children at all ages (including early adolescents) should develop the reading habit—reading aloud as an evening ritual, but also reading themselves. The more children see adults reading, the more they will also read. Reading today includes downloading from the Net. Soon it will mean reading from a hand-sized electronic device containing more books than can comfortably fit on a shelf. Since Stephen King published his latest novel on the Net, more authors are bound to follow. Reading and computer use are about to converge, an important incentive for some children.

Parents of preschool children have a major responsibility for developing reading readiness skills, but they don't have to do anything special or difficult: all they have to do is talk to children. Pointing out signs or license plates on cars; explaining why we are going to this or that store; explaining how things are organized in a kitchen; asking children questions about what they see along a street, or on a bus or subway car; asking why the child liked or disliked a television program; simply talking to children as if they were other adults—these are the bedrock of reading and of the thinking skills so necessary for success in reaching standards.

Parents cannot regard education as the responsibility of the school alone. They have to be full partners for the sake of their children.

SUSTAINING REFORM

The standards movement that began in the early 1990s has become the dominant strategy for improving schools as we turn the corner to the new century. It hasn't been easy. The movement was nearly annihilated at its inception in the firestorm over outcomes-based education and perceived threats to local control. Standards survived the conflagration only to be caught in the crossfire of the math and reading wars. The year 2000 is noteworthy for a creeping backlash by middle-class parents fearful of high-stakes testing.

Despite the ups and downs, standards have emerged with widespread acceptance. Battles continue to be fought, however, over the details. Finding the right balance between stakes for students and consequences for schools seems to inspire the most disagreement. There are also various controversies over specific curricula and philosophies. In a democracy these debates will always be with us. However, we cannot allow them to cause our unprecedented focus on high standards for all children to falter.

Sustaining the reform that has only now begun in earnest is our greatest challenge. Already we have watched as new governors, school boards, and superintendents have undone the work of their predecessors and announced they would be establishing their own standards. The loss of continuity has been a tremendous setback for students who are pulled back and forth between different philosophies before they get started. One thing we hope we have shown in this book is that standards can accommodate various approaches. As long as we maintain the focus on agreed-upon academic goals, students will meet higher achievement levels than we have ever seen before.

Elementary schools are the most hopeful environment for truly making U.S. education work for all children. They have been the first to incorporate standards and assessments into their teaching. The adults who choose elementary education as their vocation are also the most committed to children's well-being. As a result, elementary schoolchildren are beginning to show improvement in math and reading scores, even while secondary students' scores remain flat. In the first states to implement accountability systems, overall performance is increasing while some gaps between groups of students are narrowing.

More results like these show up every day. Such progress can only increase public support for staying the course. Secondary schools will find they have to change in order to handle all the bright, knowledgeable, eager students we are sending them from our reformed elementary schools.

A strong foundation in elementary school will carry our young students successfully through middle and high school. Indeed, it is our obligation as a democratic society to provide all children with this smart start.

NOTES

1. Quoted in the Spring 2000 newsletter of the Summit Education Initiative (vol. 3, no. 2, 3.)

APPENDIX A

HOW TO RECOGNIZE A GOOD ELEMENTARY SCHOOL

J UST AS WE did in the first edition of *Smart Start,* we provide here a checklist for parents, school-board members, community representatives, legislators and their staffs, and press and media to use in assessing the quality of education in elementary schools.

1. *Standards are prominently displayed in the school.* In each classroom, rubrics and scoring guides are on the walls, obviously written by and for the children because the descriptions refer to "my paper" and "my work."

2. *Each teacher can explain what standard the children's work is aligned with.* This does not mean that the teacher announces the standard at the beginning of each lesson, or that the children can recite the standard, but it does mean that the teacher can explain the reasons for the work in terms of the knowledge and skills required by the appropriate standard.

3. *The standards have been written accessibly and explained for parents, and have been distributed to them in other languages where necessary.*[1]

4. *All work in the school's classrooms is on grade level according to the standards.*

5. *Students in kindergarten can read simple books and can write, albeit with creative spelling.* In every classroom children are reading and writing constantly. Some worksheets are used, but only temporarily to reinforce skills.

6. *In each classroom, various activities are going on.* Children are working on computers, sitting in circles around adults, working quietly at tables, reading to each other, and editing each other's writing in quiet conversation. The room is not silent, but the noise is focused and purposeful, like that of a busy office.

7. *All the teachers and administrators in the school know and can tell a visitor the data about the school.* In addition to the socioeconomic data about the school's population, including the number of children eligible for Title 1 funds, teachers know the test scores for the school, broken out according to racial and economic groups. Administrators and teachers have participated in meetings with parents to discuss the test data.

8. *Teachers meet at least once a week to discuss their work.* The schedule is arranged so that teachers meet in vertical teams (one from each grade level, K–6) and horizontal teams (all the teachers of one grade level) to look at their assignments, align them with standards and with the work of other teachers, check students' work to see how they are succeeding, and exchange ideas for more effective teaching. No discussion of logistical matters (lunch duty, vending machines, field trips) is permitted at these meetings, which must be devoted to the academic core of schooling. Most of the announcements that the principal needs to make are communicated by e-mail, as all teachers are connected to each other, the administration, and the central office by e-mail.

9. *The school has plans to raise the achievement of all the students.* Whether working on a School Improvement Plan for Title 1 or as members of the School Leadership Team (or its equivalent), the school personnel have clear ideas about how the school is going to guarantee that all students will meet the standards.

10. *Groups in the school are temporary—tracking is unknown.* Children frequently break into ability groups, especially in English/language arts and mathematics, but they are assessed frequently and the groups are reconstituted as children gain skills.

11. *The school is embedded in a community support system for students.* Parents, grandparents, and members of community groups are in the school before school in the morning, during school in a dedicated community-parent room, after school, and on Saturdays to help children read, write, and learn mathematics. They have been trained as tutors by faculty from a local institution of higher education so they know how to support the teachers' work effectively.

12. *Every classroom has enough computers for one between every two students, and students take home laptops for homework.* The school can call on a trained technician from the district's central office to keep the computers running. The students routinely use the Internet for research, with their teachers' guidance.

13. *The school communicates with parents through every possible channel.* Each teacher sends an e-mail to parents about the homework assigned to students. Each teacher also has a voice mailbox at the school where parents can leave messages and hear about the assigned homework. The superintendent has a regular weekly column in the local newspaper to explain developments at the school. Report cards are not sent home or even mailed—they are delivered to the parents in person, either in parent conferences or by teachers going to students' homes. All newsletters and announcements of meetings are translated into the languages spoken by parents.

14. *Extra time is scheduled for students who need it.* Because students must have met the standards by the time they leave elementary school for middle or junior high school, and to avoid retaining students in grades beyond the appropriate age, students who show signs of difficulty are given extra time. The extra time may include time before and after school with teachers and tutors, Saturday school, summer school, and even an extra week of preparation before school starts in August or September.[2]

NOTES

1. In the Los Angeles Unified School District (LAUSD), standards were translated into four other languages besides English for the benefit of parents—Spanish, Mandarin, Korean, and Armenian.

2. The Knowledge is Power Project academies in the Bronx, New York, and Houston, Texas, lengthen the school day and the school year for their students, who are predominantly poor and minority, with spectacular results.

APPENDIX B

THE LANGUAGE OF STANDARDS

I N CHAPTER TWO we discussed the history of standards. We did not want to go so deeply into the subject of standards and the terms used to describe them that we risked losing the connection with elementary education. But "standards language" can baffle those who would like to understand the subject in detail. We have therefore listed here the terms most commonly used and illustrated them with examples where possible.

WHAT ARE CONTENT STANDARDS, PERFORMANCE STANDARDS, BENCHMARKS, RUBRICS, AND SCORING GUIDES?

As we approach definitions, we should clearly warn readers: there is no consensus nationally on exactly what the terms in the standards movement mean. For example, *benchmarks,* a term imported from the Total Quality Movement (TQM) in the business world, can mean detailed, usually bulleted, specifications printed under standards statements; or *benchmarks* can mean the stages on the way to standards at grades 4, 8, and 10.

Other examples: the expression "performance standards" has been al-most hopelessly confused by the title of the *New Standards Performance Standards,* because the books in fact contain content standards.[1] Rubrics and scoring guides are not the same thing, although the terms are often used interchangeably.

What we lay out here are definitions that we think work most effec-tively. Where possible, metaphors and examples are used for clarification.

Content or Academic Standards

These are statements of expectations about what students should know and be able to do after specified periods of schooling, at grades 4, 8, 12, for example. They are what people usually mean when they refer to *stan-dards.* Synonyms for *standards* in this sense are the words *expectations, goals, results,* and *outcomes,* although the latter word has become unus-able in this context because of its associations with outcomes-based edu-cation, which was so viciously attacked (and indeed, wiped out) by religious conservatives in the late 1980s.[2]

Standards are published statements at the national, state, and local levels. They were at first called content standards until disputes arose over whether *content* means only "knowledge" or whether it also in-cludes skill, as the standards were intended to specify what students should know *and* be able to do. The expression "academic standards" makes clear that both are included.

Standards of this kind are familiar to us in our daily lives. In the super-market, beef is sold with a series of grades stamped on it—Prime, Grade A, and so on. These are standards for the quality of beef. To get the highest grade, the beef must be judged to meet agreed-on criteria. The meat is not judged against other sides of beef in the delivery that day. If that were the case, the cut of meat could be the best in that delivery but still cause outbreaks of botulism or be as tough as shoe leather. It must meet the clear written and illustrated standards for the quality of beef. There are similar standards for electrical equipment and plumbing sup-plies. The Good Housekeeping Seal of Approval is awarded when a prod-uct meets the defined standards.

Performance Standards

These are descriptions of levels of achievement necessary to meet the standards. Academic standards define WHAT students must know and be able to do. Performance standards define HOW WELL they must do it. They must designate levels: what work looks like if it meets the standards, if it's almost there, if it needs a lot of work to make it, or if it shows clear evidence that reteaching is needed. This descending scale obviously has four points, but performance standards can be written with other configurations, three, six, even eight points. At each point, the performance standard must provide a full description of work that merits the point.

Please see the example of performance standards for writing on pages 168–169.

Benchmarks

As we said above, there are least two definitions of this word. The statements bulleted under the standards are called benchmarks in some state and city content standards. The second (and perhaps more appropriate) use of benchmarks is explicitly connected with time. In TQM parlance, benchmarks are interim goals marking progress to the major target.

The word often describes the grades on the way to the attainment of the standards at grade 12. Standards at grade 4 and 8 are in that sense benchmarks, although they are often called standards.

But teachers found the span of years between the benchmarks too great. Teachers of kindergarten and grades 1, 2, and 3 could not easily envision where students should be on the way to the big barrier at grade 4, where students had to achieve standards or be unable to move to grade 5. Responding to teachers' needs, states and local authorities have been providing grade-by-grade benchmarks.[3]

A word of caution is necessary here. Grade-by-grade standards or benchmarks threaten a major effect of standards-based education. Here's why: setting benchmarks or standards at grades 4 and 8 provided an opportunity for reform that may be lost if benchmarks are imposed on each grade level. Developmental psychologists are clear that children develop at different speeds: some are ready to read by the end of kindergarten, some not until second grade—and the variation is normal.

Examples of Performance Standards

Performance Levels (Full) Writing

Level 6
Student performances at this level are creative and effective responses to a variety of writing tasks. The writing is confident, purposeful, and clearly focused, conveying the knowledge, values, insights, and clarity of thought of the writer. The writing is skillfully adapted to its audience, purpose, and subject, is coherent throughout, and effectively captures and holds the reader's attention. An appropriate tone is established, and the work employs language that is clear, distinct, varied, and precise. Ideas are supported with appropriate reasons and well-chosen examples or details, moving smoothly from the particular to the general and from the general to the particular. A variety of sentence structures enhance the writing style, and the conventions of grammar, punctuation, capitalization, and spelling are used skillfully with few if any errors.

Level 5
Student performances at this level respond effectively to a variety of writing tasks. The writing is purposeful and focused, clearly communicating the writer's knowledge, insights, and values as well as demonstrating an understanding of audience, purpose, and subject. An appropriate tone is established in the writing, effectively engaging the reader's attention. Ideas are supported with relevant reasons, examples, or details, and the writing moves easily from the particular to the general and from the general to the particular. The writing is coherent throughout, organized effectively, and its style is enhanced with a variety of sentence structures. The writing reflects good control of the conventions of grammar, punctuation, capitalization, and spelling, with few errors.

Level 4
Student performances at this level are responsive to the demands of a variety of writing tasks. The writing generally communicates the knowledge, insights, and values of the writer. Writing at this level is appropriately adapted to its particular audience, purpose, and subject, and usually meets the reader's expectations. It is coherent and adequately organized and developed, with some ideas supported by reasons, examples, and details. The language chosen is suitable for its task, and some variety of sentence structures is employed. Although there may be occasional errors, the writing reflects adequate control of the conventions of grammar, punctuation, capitalization, and spelling.

Level 3
Student performances at this level respond inconsistently to the demands of a variety of writing tasks. All parts of the tasks are addressed, but the writing reveals little awareness of the reader. While the writing may contain some insights, it is, at times, confused, superficial, or illogical, and the communication of the writer's ideas, knowledge, and values is limited. The writing often needs additional development, and contains predictable vocabulary with some inappropriate choices of words. Repetitive sentence structures are typical of this writing level, as are unfocused collections of generalizations. Noticeable errors in the use of the conventions of grammar, punctuation, capitalization, and spelling may divert the reader's attention or cause confusion.

Level 2
Student performances at this level only partially meet the demands of writing tasks. All or parts of the tasks are addressed, but the writing shows lapses in coherence. The communication of the writer's knowledge and values is seriously impeded. The writing is typically brief, disorganized, and undeveloped and may be vague and difficult to understand. It demonstrates only limited use of language to express ideas, and contains frequent errors in the use of the conventions of grammar, punctuation, capitalization, and spelling that may slow or stop the reader.

Level I
Student performances at this level do not meet the demands of writing tasks. The writing exhibits little or no concept of audience, and the communication of the writer's knowledge and values is extremely limited. The writing is brief, incoherent, disorganized, and undeveloped and provides evidence of only a rudimentary use of language. The writing shows minimal control of the conventions of grammar, punctuation, capitalization, and spelling and may contain errors in every sentence.

The school year rests on an artificial division of time, nine months, still conforming to the agricultural lifestyle that this country abandoned during the twentieth century.[4] Children do not uniformly develop at the same speed during those nine months. But setting benchmarks at each grade level assumes that they do, and the opportunity for flexibility according to individual students' needs is lost. Grade-level standards keep us right where we are instead of permitting the innovative use of time many, perhaps most, children need.

If grade-level standards are treated as advisory, then the danger is lessened. Children can be taught in "split" classes—grades 1 and 2, or 2 and 3, for example—with the same teacher, allowing gradual transition rather than abrupt judgment at the end of each year. But if the system hardens in place with the administration of tests at every grade level, then the standards movement will not benefit all children as it promised to do. Worse, the children who will do poorly on the yearly tests will be the same children who have always failed in the U.S. system—the poor, minorities, immigrants, and speakers of other languages.

Rubrics and
Scoring Guides

Rubrics are general descriptions of levels of performance. In practice, they differ little from performance standards. Rubrics describe levels of performance across a set or class of tasks, regardless of what the specific assignment might be. For example, a rubric could be used to score persuasive writing, although the persuasive assignments might range from writing a letter to persuade the school principal to institute a recycling program to an editorial endorsing a political candidate. The rubric would describe those features that any successful written persuasion must have.

Here's an example of a rubric used in the state of Florida to score answers on questions about reading passages at grade 4:

FCAT READING
Rubric for
Short-Answer Questions

2 points   _____ **complete** understanding

             _____ **accurate** and **complete** response

             _____ **necessary** supporting details
                    and/or examples

1 point   _____ **partial** understanding

             _____ correct information but it is **too
                    general** or **simplistic**

             _____ **few** supporting details and/or
                    examples

0 points   _____ **no** understanding (inaccurate
                    answer)

             _____ **confused, no focus** (irrelevant)

             _____ no answer

FCAT READING
Rubric for
Long-Answer Questions

4 points   _____ a **deep** understanding
_____ **very accurate** and **complete** response
_____ **necessary** supporting details
and/or examples
_____ **very** focused

3 points   _____ an understanding of text
_____ accurate response
_____ **some** supporting details
_____ **some** focus

2 points   _____ **partial** understanding
_____ correct response but it is **too general**
or **simplistic**
_____ **very few or no** supporting details
and/or examples

1 point   _____ **very little** understanding
_____ **incomplete** answer with a **lot of mistakes**

0 points   _____ **no** understanding (**inaccurate** answer)
_____ **confused, no focus** (irrelevant)
_____ no answer

A scoring guide, on the other hand, relates to the assigned task. It describes what responses to that assignment would look like: its wording refers, for example, to the kinds of arguments that would persuade the principal, or the specific reasons why the political candidate deserves support.

Here's what a scoring guide would look like for the performance assessment example we used in chapter seven (the "dots" problem):

For a score of 4: *The student work is characterized by a confident understanding of pattern and how to explain a solution.*

- It extends the linear pattern by rule.

- It shows correct computation.

- There is a clear and logical explanation, illustrated with a diagram, that another student could follow, extend the linear pattern, and get the correct answer.

For a score of 3: *The student work is accurate and shows understanding.*

- It extends the linear pattern by rule.

- It shows correct computation.

- There is a clear explanation.

For a score of 2: *The student work shows some understanding.*

- It attempts to extend the linear pattern.

- It may have computational errors.

- It attempts an explanation *or* it has a solution but no explanation.

For a score of 1: *The student work shows little understanding.*

- It attempts a solution.

- There may a minimal or unclear explanation, or none at all.

It is through scoring guides that elementary students can understand standards. In a Pueblo, Colorado, elementary school in 1995, teachers who had learned to construct scoring guides as part of professional development workshops asked their students to help. They described an assignment and then asked the children what a really good answer would look like, one that made them exclaim, "Wow!" As the children brainstormed the answer, the teachers wrote their responses in "kid language," that is, in the first person using elementary-level vocabulary.

The idea spread throughout the school until all the classrooms, even kindergarten, had their own scoring guides. Teachers began to notice that students whom they had thought of as low-performing did better: the students could see in front of them what they were expected to do. Students who had always done well found it a bit harder to earn As easily, because they had to fulfill all the details of the "Wow!" level. Teachers found that they could justify their grades to the students and to their parents by referring to the scoring guide displayed on the classroom wall.

An observer in another school saw a kindergartner walking up to the teacher's desk to deposit his work. The child stopped on the way, looked at the scoring guide, said "It isn't a 4 yet," and turned back to his desk to revise his work.

Scoring guides written jointly by students and teachers are now fairly widespread, although more commonly found in elementary school than at the secondary levels. The value of involving children in responsibility for their own learning can hardly be overestimated. Scoring guides show them how to set goals for themselves and in doing so, reach the level of learning they will need for their lives.

NOTES

1. Performance standards have levels, but the *New Standards Performance Standards* do not include levels of achievement, although they do include examples of student work that meets standards.

2. Curiously, the word *outcomes* is preferable in the world of postsecondary education, which prefers it to *standards,* meaning "admissions standards" for postsecondary administration and faculty.

3. The New Standards Primary Literacy Committee has recently produced grade-by-grade standards for literacy: *Reading and Writing Grade by Grade: Primary Literacy Standards for Kindergarten Through Third Grade*. The book is accompanied by CD-ROMs for reading and for writing.

4. Even year-round schooling on the whole does not increase the number of days in school. Year-round schools divide the year up differently (only a few weeks off in the summer, for example), but the total year is still about nine months long.

APPENDIX C

STANDARDS FOR THE ARTS AND WORLD LANGUAGES

THE FIRST EDITION of *Smart Start* included standards for the arts and languages in addition to English. We did not discuss them in chapter two because we wanted to focus on the central core of the curriculum there. But many people quite reasonably think of the arts as the core of elementary education. Additional languages are rarely championed with the same fervor, but they too seem important at the elementary level.

However, despite our profound desire that things should be different, the main thrust of elementary school must be literacy and the development of reasoning skills as taught by mathematics and science, especially for poor and minority children. Until children can all read fluently by third grade and are ready for algebra at the end of sixth grade, the arts and additional languages must be pursued outside school hours. The hours in school must focus on essential skills.

This does not mean that children will not experience art or begin to hear and speak other languages. Extended day programs can provide these experiences. Indeed, the school day, the school week, and the school year are being extended in many districts as it becomes abundantly clear that the present daily and yearly calendars are based on ways of living—the agricultural cycle, for one—that were left behind in the mid-twentieth century.

In addition, at least in the case of the arts, and to some extent with additional languages, knowledge about them can be incorporated into reading, literature, history, and geography. Observing closely and drawing exactly what is seen—as opposed to what was expected—is an activity equally valid in science and visual arts, for example, as we said in chapter three.

Most state tests do not include the arts and languages, so that, human nature being as it is, they will not be included in the curriculum to the same degree as the four core subjects.[1] However, because both the arts and languages are important for a complete education, we have listed here the standards in both.

THE ARTS, GRADES 4 AND 6

Standards documents at the state and national levels have no separate standards for the arts at grade 1, with the exception of music, which has standards for K–2. The other three arts begin with standards at the K–4 level. Following the practice of Kendall and Marzano in *Content Knowledge*, we have listed standards for grade 1 only in music.

Although the national standards for the arts are divided into sections for dance, music, theater, and visual arts, they have five underlying principles that apply at all levels:

1. Students should be able to communicate at a basic level in dance, music, theater, and the visual arts. That is, they should know the basic tools and techniques of each discipline.

2. They should be able to communicate proficiently in one of the four art forms.

3. They should be able to analyze works of art in all four disciplines from the perspectives of structure, history, and culture.

4. They should know and recognize exemplary works of art in all four disciplines from a variety of cultural backgrounds and historical periods.

5. They should be able to relate the arts across the four disciplines in cultural and historical contexts.

Music Standards, Grade 1

Students can sing repetitions of a musical pattern, partner songs, and rounds; repeat short rhythms accurately; use sounds of all kinds to make music, including clapping, stamping, banging, and electronic sounds; know the standard symbols of written music; and can recognize music of different cultures and for different purposes.

Dance Standards, Grade 4

By the end of grade 4, students should be able to demonstrate fundamental locomotor and axial movements basic to choreography; create dance sequences; perform folk dances; and be able to discuss dance as a form of expression in different cultures.

Music Standards, Grade 4

Students should be able to sing independently and with others on pitch and in rhythm; play an instrument alone or with others on pitch and in rhythm; read and compose music; improvise simple tunes and songs; evaluate music performances; and identify musical styles in various historical periods and cultures.

Theater Standards,
Grade 4

Students should be able to dramatize improvisations based on their reading in literature and history; act, direct, and design these classroom improvisations; and be able to compare and contrast theater, film, television, and electronic media as forms of drama.

Visual Arts Standards,
Grade 4

Students will know the differences among various materials, techniques, and processes (two-dimensional, three-dimensional, paints, crayons, black-and-white drawings, etc.) and describe the different effects of each; select subjects and use them to convey meaning; and understand the purposes of the visual arts in various cultures and periods of history.

Dance Standards,
Grade 6

By the time students graduate from elementary school, they understand choreographic principles and structures so that they can create a dance and solve the movement problems presented by their idea; they can evaluate dance performances; perform folk, classical, and social dances from various cultures; and understand the context of the dances.

Music Standards,
Grade 6

Students can sing accurately and with good breath control a repertory of songs of appropriate difficulty; play at least one instrument with the same degree of technical proficiency; improvise accompaniments and short melodies; compose and arrange using traditional methods and electronic media; read at sight simple melodies in treble and bass clefs; and describe the distinguishing characteristics of musical genres and styles from a variety of cultures.

Theater Standards,
Grade 6

Students can write, act, design, and direct both improvised and scripted scenes, using their personal experience and their reading in literature and history; incorporate other art forms into their dramatic presentations (dance, music, visual arts); and account for the dramatic effect of an author's or director's choices.

Visual Arts Standards,
Grade 6

Students select the most effective media and techniques for what they intend to express and can explain their choices; can describe multiple purposes for creating works of art; and compare the characteristics of two artworks concerned with similar subject matter across historical periods and cultures.

These statements from the nationally published arts standards are adequate to describe expectations, but they were written by committees whose members were forced into circumspect language in order to avoid offense to competing interests. As descriptions of experience in the arts for elementary students, we much prefer what we wrote in the first edition of *Smart Start* in 1991. We have therefore included our statements here, in hopes to inspire elementary teachers, administrators, and parents.

By the time they leave elementary school, children will have had the following experiences in the arts:

- *Studio instruction.* This means that they will not simply have been given permission to "express themselves" in paint, with clay, or in free-form dance. They will have been taught principles of drawing, musical notation, elementary stagecraft, and fundamental patterns and steps in ballet and folk dancing.

- *Exposure to professional performances and exhibitions,* with careful preparation in the classroom and extensive written reactions afterward.

- *Instruction in the history of art* in the periods, times, and places they study in history, geography, and literature.

- *Instruction in criticism and aesthetics.* Why do you think this is beautiful? Why does it move you? What makes one dance better than another, or one play more effective than another? What patterns can you discern in this painting or this piece of music?

- *Experience in using technology* for artistic expression, not merely to record performances. This includes electronic music (many students will have synthesizers in their homes), video and neon art, multimedia experiences, and performance art.

They will also have specific knowledge of each major art form.

In *music,* they will be able to identify major differences in musical styles from different cultures, recognizing typical sounds and instruments; they will be able to characterize the major styles of European music, from the Renaissance through the great Romantic composers; they will be able to identify a symphony, a concerto, and an opera; and they will know the instruments of the orchestra.

In *visual and plastic arts,* they will recognize major stylistic differences among the major cultures so that they could be expected to identify a Japanese landscape, a Native American totem, and a Greek sculpture, for example. These will be tied to the world history/geography they have studied. They will also be able to recognize and place in the correct historical context the major trends of European art, such as Renaissance portraits, eighteenth-century landscapes, Impressionism, and modernism. For example, no student leaving elementary school should be ignorant of the *Mona Lisa* or Picasso's *Guernica*.

For both *theater and dance,* they should know the development of theater and its various forms, from the amphitheaters of Greece through the thrusting Renaissance stage to the proscenium of the nineteenth century. They should know what kinds of performances are characteristic of the civilizations they study in world history. Technology lends a hand here: videotapes of Noh plays and Greek tragedies should be available in the school's media center.

In *dance,* they will understand major styles and the body concepts they are based on—the extended toe of classical European ballet, the flexed foot of Hindu dances, the fluid rhythm of jazz dancing, and the percussion of tap dancing.

ADDITIONAL LANGUAGES, GRADES 4 AND 6

Like the arts, standards for foreign languages (as they are called in the standards documents) have no benchmarks for grades below 4.

The national standards for foreign languages are divided into five sections, each of which has two or three standards under it. The five divisions are known as the Five Cs. They are:

1. *Communication:* the ability to communicate in languages other than English. It is important to note that communication is the objective of foreign language learning, as opposed to learning the structure of the language, its syntax, vocabulary, and idiom.

2. *Cultures:* knowing and understanding the culture of other countries.

3. *Connections:* using the foreign language to learn other disciplines and to understand the culture of the country by using the target language.

4. *Comparisons:* comparing the structure of the target language with that of one's own language in order to understand how language works.

5. *Communities:* using the language to become part of a community of speakers, including e-mail and the Internet.

Additional Languages Standards, Grade 4

Students can ask questions in the target language about family, events, likes and dislikes, and can conduct routine social interactions, such as greeting, leave-taking, and following simple directions, with the appropriate cultural gestures and behavior; understand the main ideas in oral and written narratives, posters, and advertisements; repeat children's songs; notice differences and similarities between their native and the target language in idiomatic usage; have pen (or e-mail) pals with whom they communicate in the target language.

Additional Languages
Standards, Grade 6

Students can express opinions and support them using the target language; ask for goods, services, and information, both orally and in writing; write stories, short plays and skits, and reports about personal and school events; watch TV, listen to the radio, and read newspapers; use the information to explain differences between cultures; and use the target language in other academic disciplines.

NOTES

1. The National Assessment of Educational Progress (NAEP), the only national test administered in this country, has assessed the arts twice in the last twenty years. NAEP has not assessed additional languages.

APPENDIX D

STANDARDS DOCUMENTS

THE FOLLOWING ARE the sources for the standards in chapter three and Appendix B.

American Association for the Advancement of Science. *Benchmarks for Scientific Literacy.* New York: Oxford University Press, 1993.

American Council on the Teaching of Foreign Languages. *Standards for Foreign Language Learning: Preparing for the 21st Century.* Lawrence, Kans.: Allen Marketing and Management, 1995.

Board of Education of the City of New York. *What Did You Learn in School Today?* Parent brochures. New York: New York City Board of Education, 1999.

Consortium of National Arts Education Associations. *National Standards for Arts Education.* Reston, Va.: Music Educators' National Conference, 1994.

Council for Basic Education. *Standards for Excellence in Education: A Guide for Parents, Teachers, and Principals for Evaluating and Implementing Standards for Education.* Washington, D.C.: Council for Basic Education, 1998.

Geography Education Standards Project. *Geography for Life: National Geography Standards 1994.* Washington, D.C.: National Geographic Research and Exploration, 1994.

Indiana Department of Education. *Indiana Academic Standards: Standards 1999.* Indianapolis: State Board of Education, 1999.

Kendall, John S., and Robert J. Marzano. *Content Knowledge: A Compendium of Standards and Benchmarks for K–12 Education.* Aurora, Colo.: Mid-Continent Regional Educational Laboratory, 1996.

National Center for History in the Schools. *National Standards for History* (basic edition). Los Angeles: University of California–Los Angeles, 1996.

————*National Standards for History for Grades K–4: Expanding Children's World in Time and Space.* Los Angeles: University of California–Los Angeles, 1994.

National Center on Education and the Economy (NCEE). *New Standards Performance Standards, Volume 1: Elementary School.* Washington, D.C.: NCEE, 1997.

National Research Council (NRC). *National Science Education Standards.* Washington, D.C.: NRC, 1996.

New Standards Primary Literacy Committee. *Reading and Writing Grade by Grade: Primary Literacy Standards for Kindergarten Through Third Grade.* Washington, D.C.: National Center on Education and the Economy, 1999.

BIBLIOGRAPHY

Adelman, Clifford. *Answers in the Tool Box*. Washington, D.C.: U.S. Department of Education, June 1999.

American Federation of Teachers (AFT). *Making Standards Matter, 1995, 1996, 1997, 1998, 1999*. Washington, D.C.: AFT annual.

American Institutes for Research (AIR). *An Educator's Guide to Schoolwide Reform*. Washington, D.C.: AIR, 1999. http://www.aasa.org/reform/intro.html.

Anderson, R.C., E.H. Hiebert, J.A. Scott, and I. Wilkinson, eds. *Becoming a Nation of Readers: The Report of the Commission on Reading*. Washington, D.C.: National Institute of Education, 1985.

Armstrong, Thomas. "ADD as a Social Invention." *Education Week* (October 18, 1995): 46.

Barth, John W., Senta Raizen, Richard Howang, William H. Schmidt, Leland Cogan, Frances Lawrenz, and Bill Linder-Scholer. "Minnesota and TIMSS: Exploring High Achievement in Eighth Grade Science." National Education Goals Panel, Washington, D.C., Autumn 2000.

Barth, Patte, and Ruth Mitchell. "Not Good Enough: A Content Analysis of Teacher Licensing Examinations." *Thinking K–16, Spring 1999*. Washington, D.C.: Education Trust, 1999.

Benning, Victoria. "Virginia School Overshoots Goal." *Washington Post* (August 11, 2000): B1.

Claiborne, William. "In Short Supply: Teachers Join Special Visa List." *Washington Post* (December 24, 1999): A1.

Committee for Economic Development (CED). *The Unfinished Agenda: A New Vision for Child Development and Education*. New York: CED, 1991.

Committee on Development in the Science of Learning. *How People Learn: Brain, Mind, Experience, and School* (expanded edition). Washington, D.C.: National Academy Press, 2000.

Education Trust. *Education Watch, Vol. II, 1998.* Washington, D.C.: Education Trust, 1998.

Education Week. *Technology Counts 98.* Washington, D.C.: Education Week, 1998.

Egan, Kieran. *Teaching as Story Telling.* Chicago: University of Chicago Press, 1989.

Farnham-Diggory, Sylvia. *Schooling.* Cambridge, Mass.: Harvard University Press, 1990.

Fatemi, Erik. "Building the Digital Curriculum: Summary." In *Technology Counts 99.* Washington, D.C.: Education Week, 1999.

Ferguson, Ronald F. "Can Schools Narrow the Black-White Test Score Gap?" In *The Black-White Test Score Gap,* edited by Christopher Jencks and Meredith Phillips. Washington, D.C.: Brookings Institution Press, 1998.

———"Paying for Public Education: New Evidence of How and Why Money Matters." *Harvard Journal of Legislation* 28 (Summer 1991): 465-498.

Fielding, Lynn, Nancy Kerr, and Paul Rosier. *The 90% Reading Goal.* Kennewick, Wash.: New Foundation Press, 1998.

Fletcher, Jack M., and G. Reid Lyon. "Reading: A Research-Based Approach." In *What's Gone Wrong in America's Classrooms?* edited by Williamson M. Evers. Stanford, Calif.: Hoover Institution Press, 1998.

Friedman, Thomas. *The Lexus and the Olive Tree.* New York: Anchor Books, 2000.

Gardner, Howard. *Frames of Mind: The Theory of Multiple Intelligences.* New York: Basic Books, 1983.

———*Intelligence Reframed: Multiple Intelligences for the 21st Century.* New York: Basic Books, 1999.

Grissmer, David, et al. *Improving Student Achievement: What NAEP Test Scores Tell Us.* Santa Monica, Calif.: RAND, 2000.

Grissmer, David, David Flanagan and Ann Flanagan. "Rapid Gains in North Carolina and Texas." National Education Goals Panel, Washington, D.C., November 1998.

Haberman, Martin. "Selecting 'Star' Teachers for Children and Youth in Urban Poverty." *Phi Delta Kappan* 74 (June 1995): 777–781.

———"Thirty-one Reasons to Stop the School Reading Machine." *Phi Delta Kappan* 74, no. 4 (1989): 284–288.

Hanushek, Eric A. "The Trade-off Between Child Quantity and Quality," *Journal of Political Economy* (1992).

Haycock, Kati. "Good Teaching Matters." *Thinking K–16* (Summer 1998).

Hodgkinson, Harold. "Reform Versus Reality." *Phi Delta Kappan* 73, no. 1 (1991): 8–16.

Hollingsworth, John, and Silvia Ybarra. *Analyzing Classroom Instruction: Curriculum Calibration.* http://www.cascd.org/analyzingin struction.html.

Jencks, Christopher, and Meredith Phillips, eds. *The Black-White Test Score Gap.* Washington, D.C.: Brookings Institution Press, 1998.

Johnson, Joseph. *Hope for Urban Schools.* Austin: Charles A. Dana Center, University of Texas-Austin, 1999.

Katz, Jon. *Geeks: How Two Lost Boys Rode the Internet Out of Idaho.* New York: Villard, 2000.

King, Dorothy F. "Real Kids or Unreal Tasks: The Obvious Choice." *Basic Education* 35, no. 2 (1990): 6–9.

Knapp, Michael S., Patrick M. Shields, and Brenda J. Turnbull. "Academic Challenge in High-Poverty Classrooms." *Phi Delta Kappan* (June 1995): 770–776.

Langer, Judith. *Guidelines for Teaching Middle and High School Students to Read and Write Well: Six Features of Effective Instruction.* Albany, N.Y.: Center on English Learning, State University of New York, 2000.

Leinwand, Steven. "It's Time to Abandon Computational Algorithms." *Education Week* (February 9, 1994): 48.

Lyon, G. Reid. Statement before the Committee of Labor and Human Resources, U.S. Senate, Washington, D.C., 1998.

Morris, Clifford. *The Midas News,* www.angelfire.com/oh/themidas-news/oct4art.html.

National Center for Education Statistics. *NAEP 1998 Reading Report.* Washington, D.C.: U.S. Department of Education, March 1999.
———*NAEP 1996 Mathematics Report Card.* Washington, D.C.: U.S. Department of Education, February 1997.

National Commission on Excellence in Education. *A Nation at Risk: The Imperative for Educational Reform, A Report to the Nation and the Secretary of Education.* Washington, D.C.: U.S. Department of Education, April 1983.

National Council on Education Standards and Testing (NCEST). *Raising Standards for American Education: A Report to Congress, the Secretary of Education, the National Education Goals Panel, and the American People.* Washington, D.C.: NCEST, 1992

National Education Commission on Time and Learning. *Prisoners of Time.* Washington, D.C.: U.S. Government Printing Office, 1994.

National Reading Panel. *Teaching Children to Read: An Evidence-Based Assessment of the Scientific Research Literature on Reading and Its Implications for Reading Instruction.* Washington, D.C: National Institute of Child Health and Human Development, 2000.

National Telecommunications and Information Administration. *Falling through the Net.* Washington, D.C.: U.S. Department of Commerce, 1999.

New Standards Primary Literacy Committee. *Reading and Writing Grade by Grade: Primary Literacy Standards for Kindergarten Through Third Grade.* Washington, D.C.: National Center on Education and the Economy, 1999.

Newmann, Fred M., and Associates. *Authentic Achievement: Restructuring Schools for Intellectual Quality.* San Francisco: Jossey-Bass, 1996.

Newmann, Fred M., Gudelia Lopez, and Anthony S. Bryk. *The Quality of Intellectual Work in Chicago Schools: A Baseline Report.* Chicago: Consortium on Chicago School Research, October 1998.

Preller, Paula. *Thoughtful Literacy in Elementary Classrooms: English.* Newsletter from the Center on English Learning and Achievement (CELA). Albany, N.Y.: SUNY, Spring 2000.

Puma, Michael, et al. *Prospects: The Congressionally Mandated Study of Educational Growth and Opportunity.* Washington, D.C.: U.S. Department of Education, 1997.

Quality Education for Minorities Project. *Education That Works: An Action Plan for the Education of Minorities.* Cambridge, Mass.: Massachusetts Institute of Technology, 1990.

Ravitch, Diane. "Tot Sociology." *American Scholar* 56, no. 3 (1987): 343-354.

Resnick, Lauren. *Education and Learning to Think.* Washington, D.C.: National Academy Press, 1987.

Rose, Mike. "An Instructional Program That's Worth Stealing." *American Teacher* 81, no. 8 (1997).

Skiba, Russ, and Reece Peterson. "The Dark Side of Zero Tolerance: Can Punishment Lead to Safe Schools?" *Phi Delta Kappan* (January 1999).

Slavin, Robert E. *Ability Grouping and Student Achievement in Elementary Schools: A Best-Evidence Synthesis.* Baltimore, Md.: Center for Research on Elementary and Middle Schools, 1986.

U.S. Department of Education. *Annual Report on School Safety— October 1998.* Washington, D.C.: National Center for Education Statistics, 1998.

———*Becoming a Nation of Readers.* Washington, D.C.: National Center for Education Statistics, 1985.

———The Condition of Education, 2000. Washington, D.C.: National Center for Education Statistics, 2000.

———Digest of Education Statistics, 1999. Washington, D.C.: National Center for Education Statistics, 1999.

———"Essay: Entering Kindergarten: A Portrait of American Children." In *The Condition of Education, 2000.* Washington, D.C.: National Center for Education Statistics, 2000. www.nces.ed.gov/pubs2000/coe2000.

———*Internet Access in U.S. Public Schools and Classrooms, 1994–1999.* Washington, D.C.: National Center for Education Statistics, 1999.

———*Long-Term Trends in Student Mathematics Performance.* Washington, D.C.: National Center for Education Statistics, 1998.

———*National Assessment of Education Progress (NAEP) 1996 National Mathematics Results, Data Almanacs for Grades 4 and 8, Student Data.* Washington, D.C.: National Center for Education Statistics, 1996. www.nces.ed.gov/nationsreport-card/tables.

———Section 4. www.nces.ed.gov/pubs2000/coe2000/section4.

———*Student Computer Use.* Washington, D.C.: National Center for Education Statistics, 1999.

"Writing Skills Key to Success on MD Tests, Kent County Says." *Washington Post* (December 13, 1999): B1.

ACKNOWLEDGMENTS

BOOKS ABOUT EDUCATION do not arise from sitting at a desk, reading, and thinking. They arise from experiences in schools and classrooms, and, in our case, from exchanges among colleagues at Education Trust staff meetings and subsequent corridor conversations. So we thank our colleagues not only for advice and support, but also for pointing us towards the schools and classrooms where we saw elementary children learning and enjoying it. We also thank the principals and teachers who allowed us to visit those schools and classrooms freely, without worrying about what we might write about them.

We are especially grateful to Kati Haycock, executive director of the Education Trust; Anne Lewis, education consultant; and Craig Jerald, Senior Policy analyst at the Education Trust, who read the manuscript of *Smart Start II* and provided the feedback we needed.

We have always received encouragement and support from our friends at Fulcrum Publishing, especially Jill Scott and Susan Zernial, and we thank them. It was a real vote of confidence to be asked to update the original *Smart Start,* now ten years old.

We thank Jon Chester for his delightful pencil drawings, bringing our elementary children to life.

And of course we thank long-suffering family members whose interests were inevitably subordinated on occasion to the demands of the book. We ask them to take the long view—elementary education shapes the future for everyone.

INDEX